Secret Worlds

Adult Coloring Book

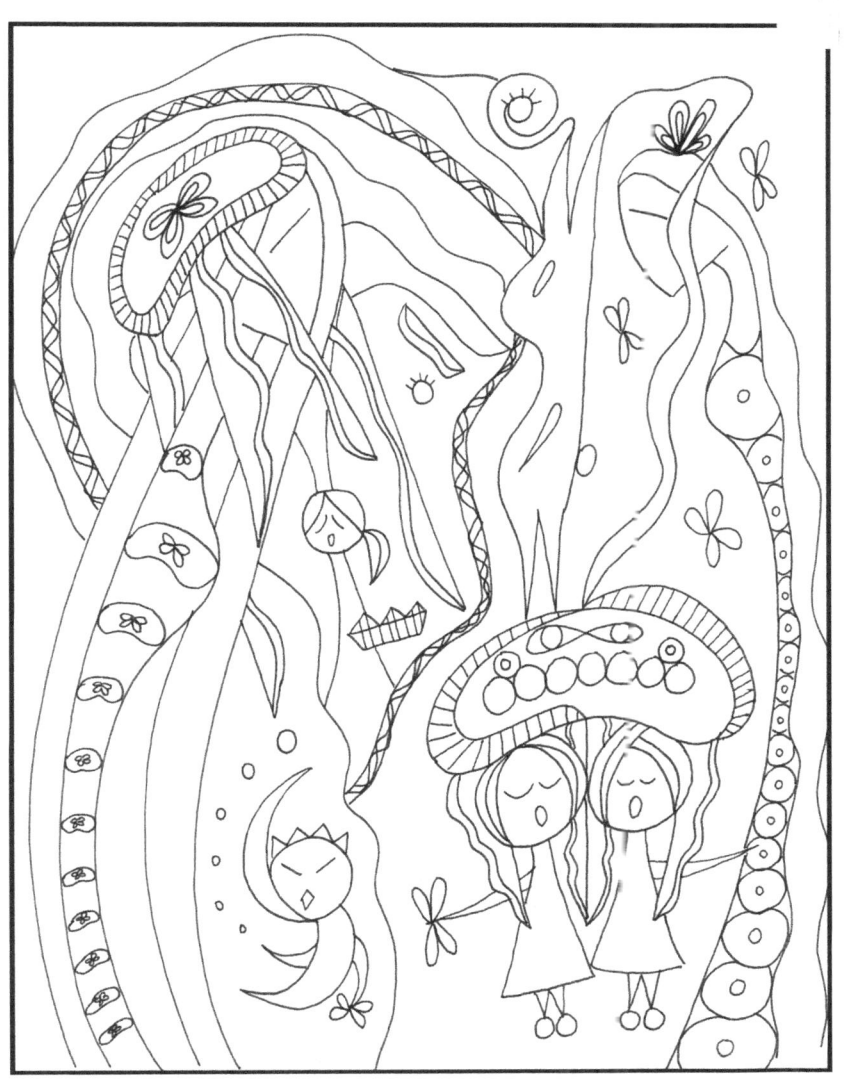

Hunter Cole

Copyright © 2020 Hunter Cole
www.HunterCole.org

  huntercolephotography

 huntercolephoto

Hunter Cole - Bio

Internationally recognized artist Hunter Cole's work includes paintings, photography, digital art, and living art using bioluminescent bacteria. The New Orleans-based artist produces work that is inspired by science, but lives as art. Cole, who holds a PhD in genetics, reinterprets science through art. Cole has taught on the science faculties of the University of Wisconsin, Loyola University Chicago, and Loyola University New Orleans.

The artist's projects have included: live performances of dancers adorned with light produced by bioluminescent bacteria; a residency at the prestigious SymbioticA laboratory at the University of Western Australia in Perth; and creating a site specific permanent installation of public art comissioned by Loyola University Chicago for its Lake Shore campus. Entitled, Biological Domains, the installation is comprised of 14 paintings and LED lighting that depict specific areas in biology.

Hunter Cole's art has been exhibited internationally including: New York, San Francisco, Chicago, the United Kingdom, Italy, Japan, and the Czech Republic. The artist has also presented numerous seminars on art and science at locations including the School of the Art Institute of Chicago (SAIC), the American Museum of Natural History (New York), Massachusetts Institute of Technology (MIT), Dialogue Between Science and Art Workshop in Hluboka, Czech Republic, and SymbioticA at the University of Western Australia in Perth, Australia. Cole has been the subject of numerous newspaper and magazine articles, including the Chicago Tribune and the New Orlean's Times-Picayune/Advocate.

For more information about the artist: www.HunterCole.org

Create Your Own Secret Worlds Title
Plate Number: 01

Submit your colorful creation
to be displayed online at
www.HunterCole.org/color

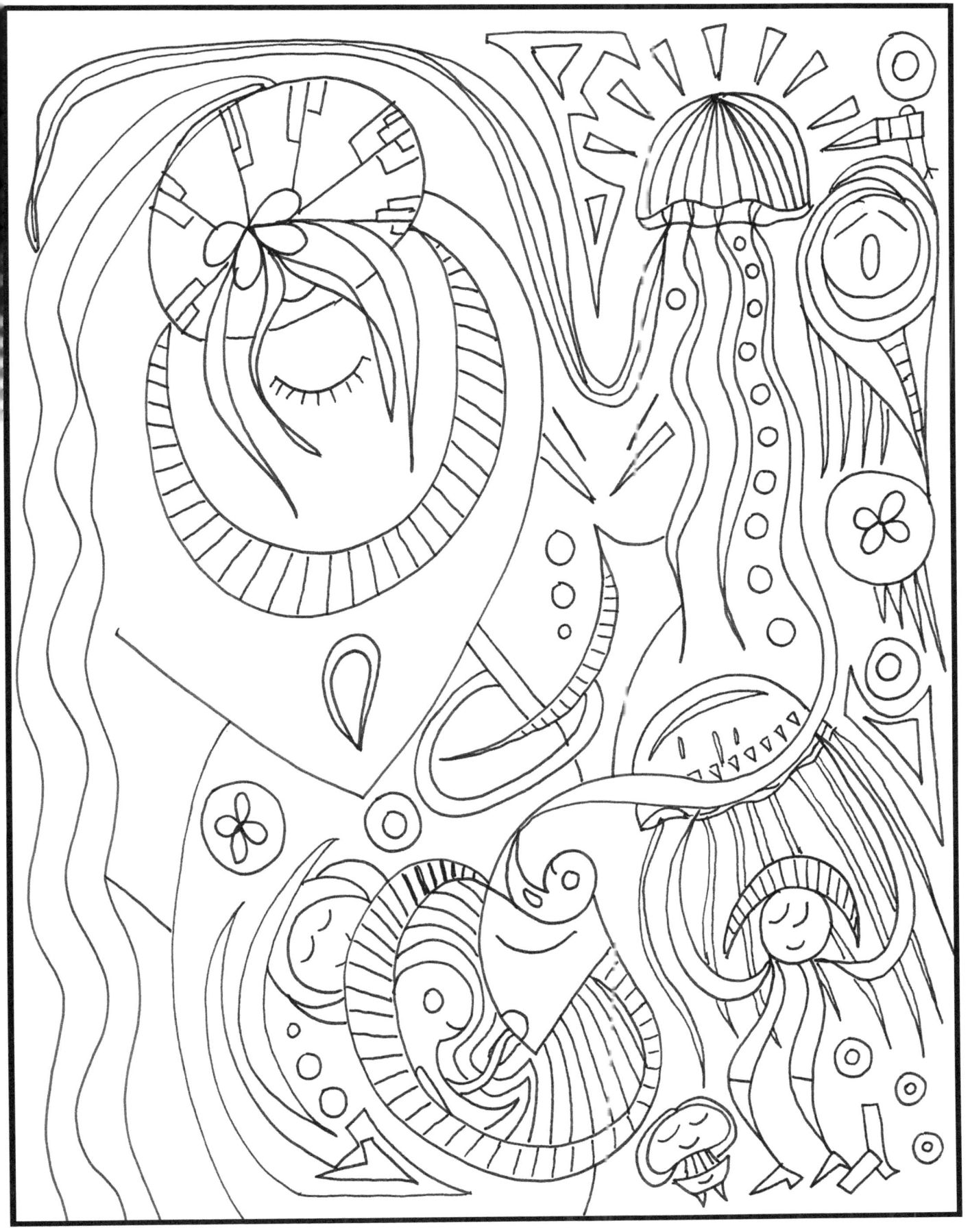

Create Your Own Secret Worlds Title
Plate Number: 02

Submit your colorful creation
to be displayed online at
www.HunterCole.org/color

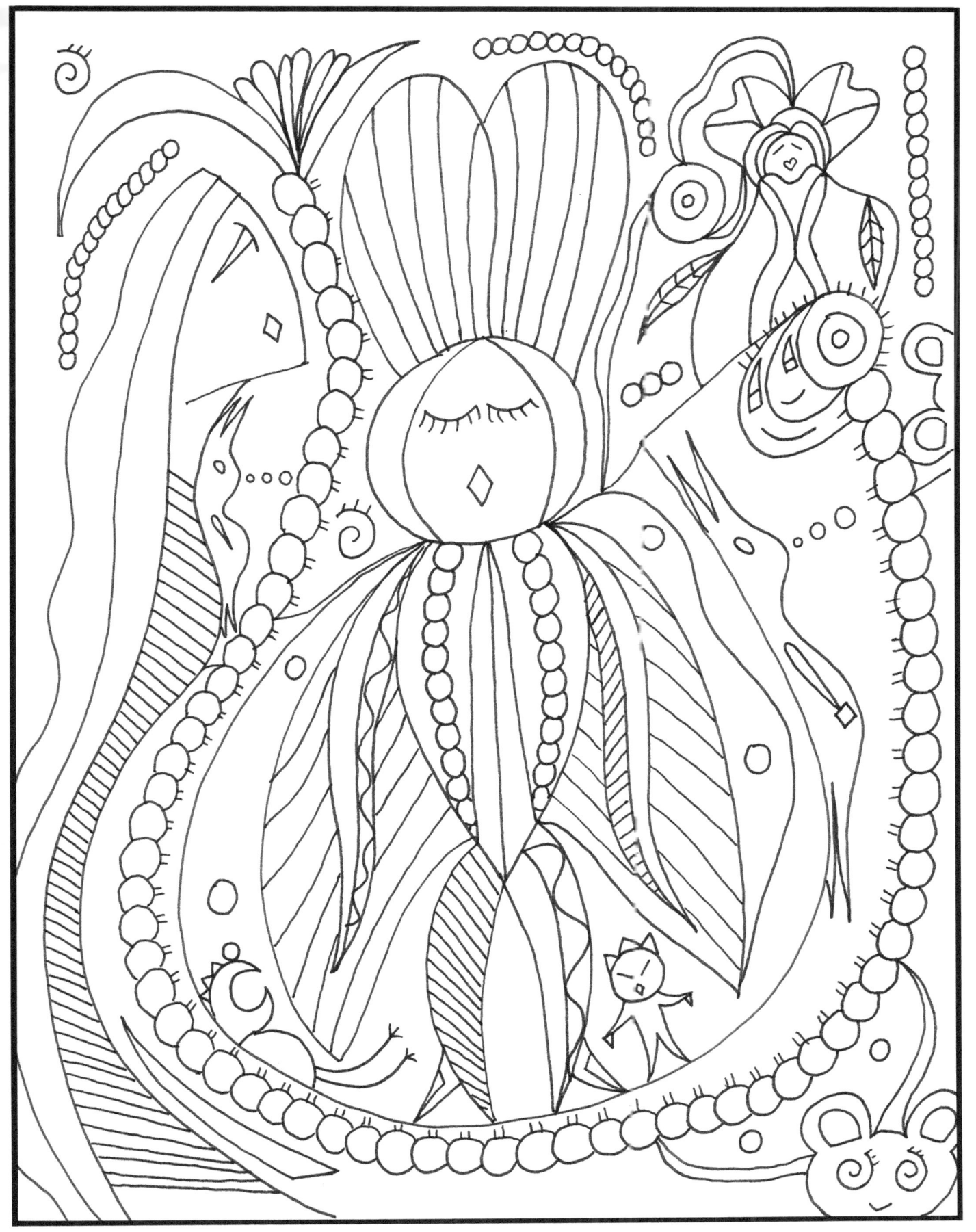

Create Your Own Secret Worlds Title
Plate Number: 03

Submit your colorful creation
to be displayed online at
www.HunterCole.org/color

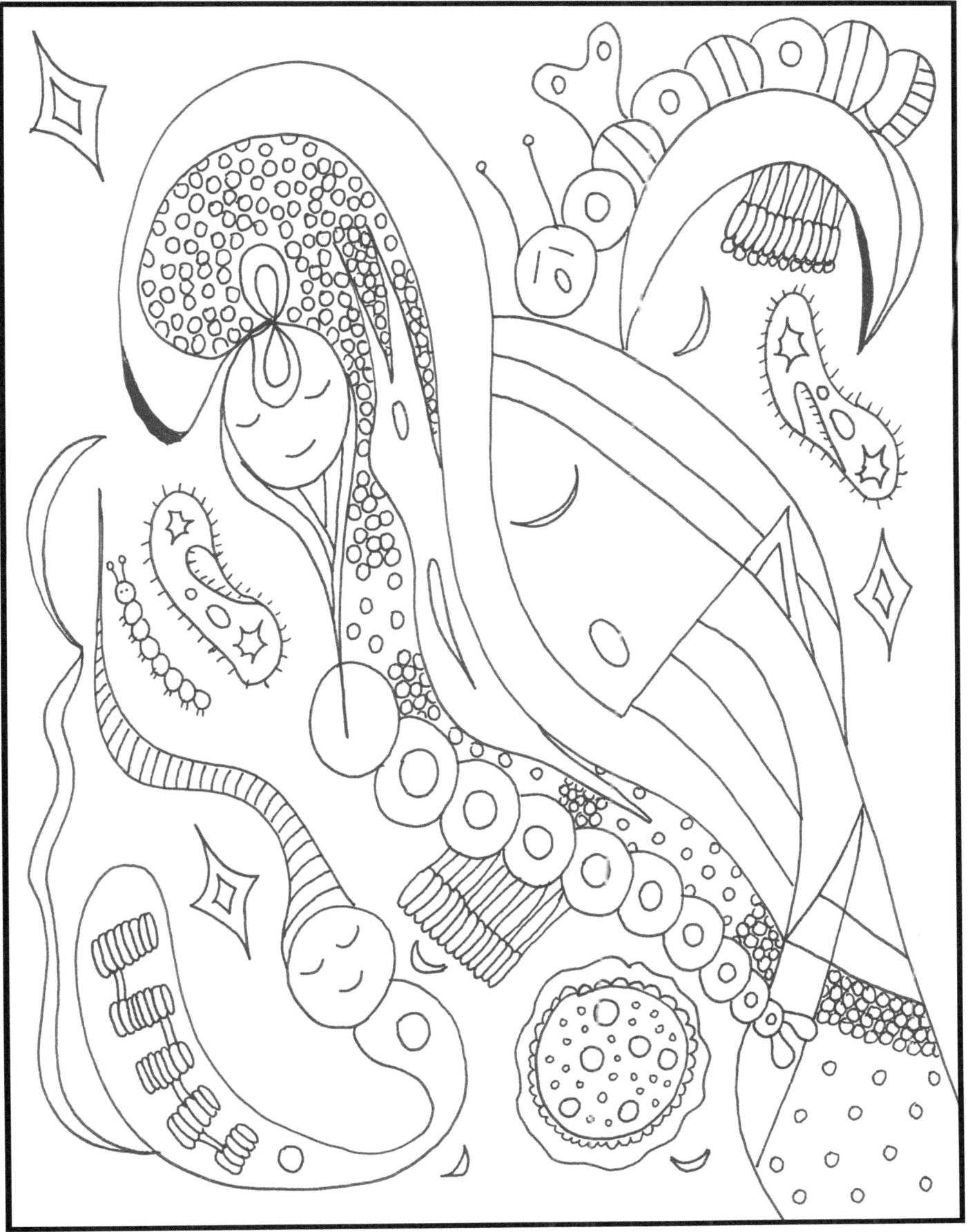

Create Your Own Secret Worlds Title
Plate Number: 04

Submit your colorful creation
to be displayed online at
www.HunterCole.org/color

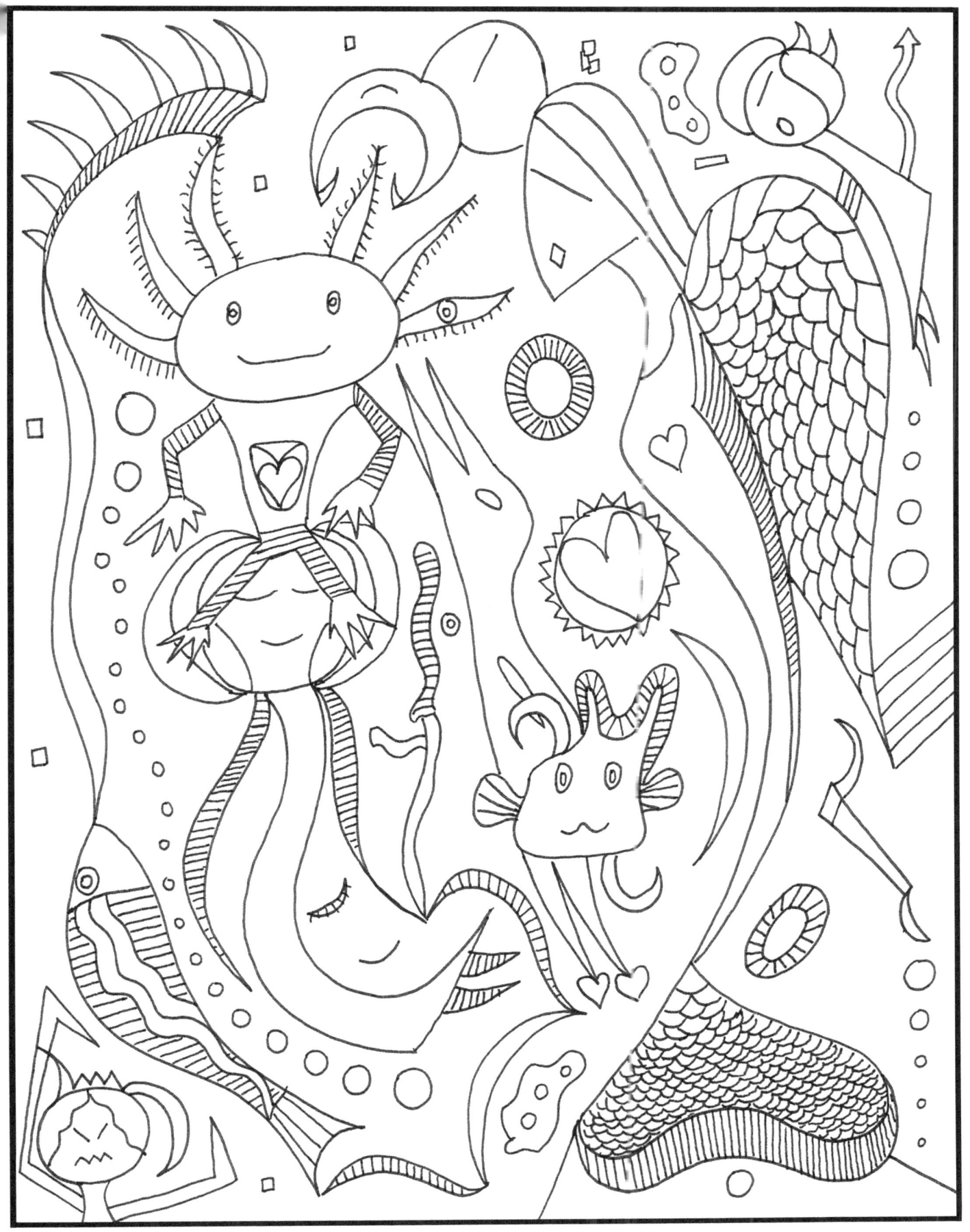

Create Your Own Secret Worlds Title
Plate Number: 05

Submit your colorful creation
to be displayed online at
www.HunterCole.org/color

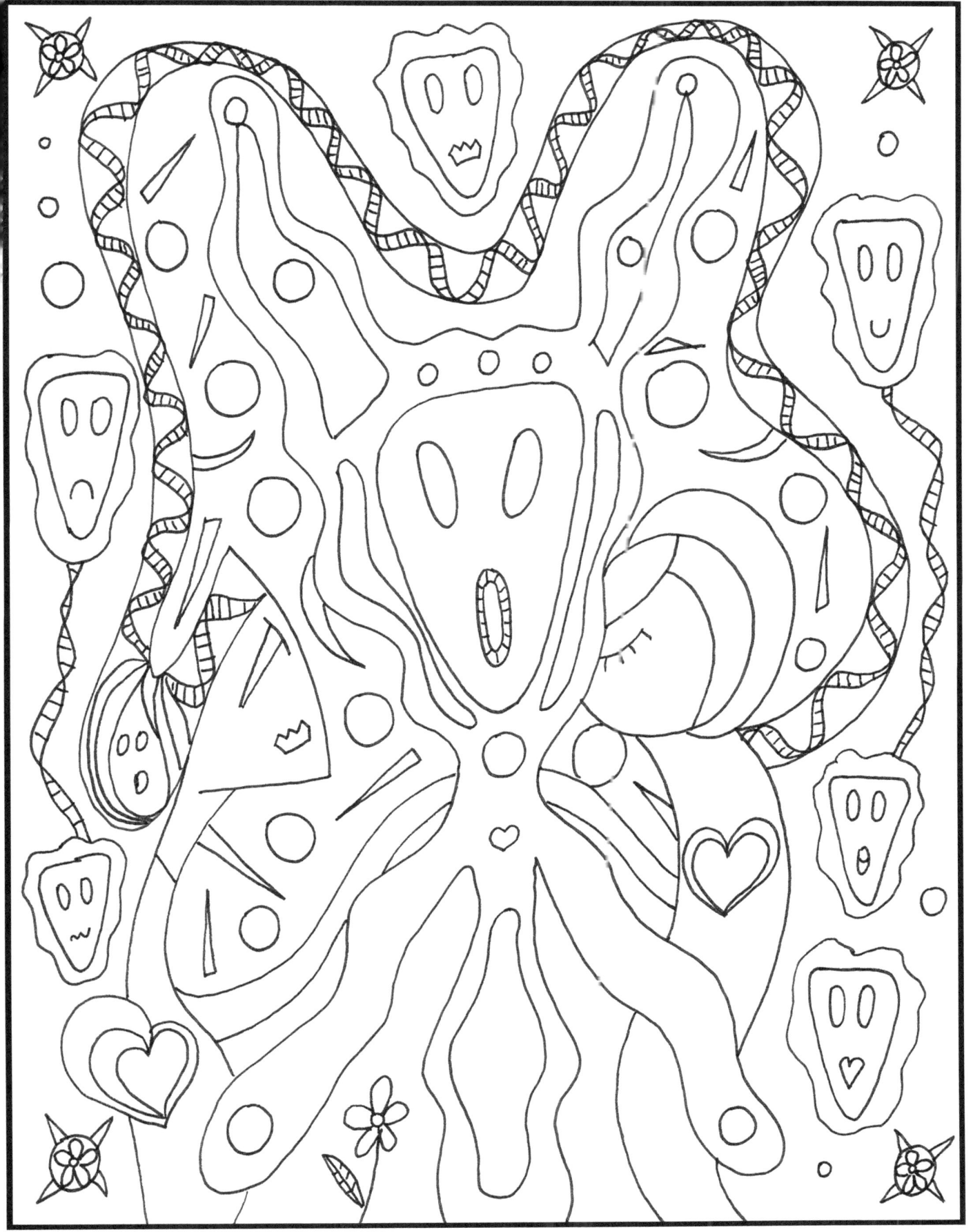

Create Your Own Secret Worlds Title
Plate Number: 06

Submit your colorful creation
to be displayed online at
www.HunterCole.org/color

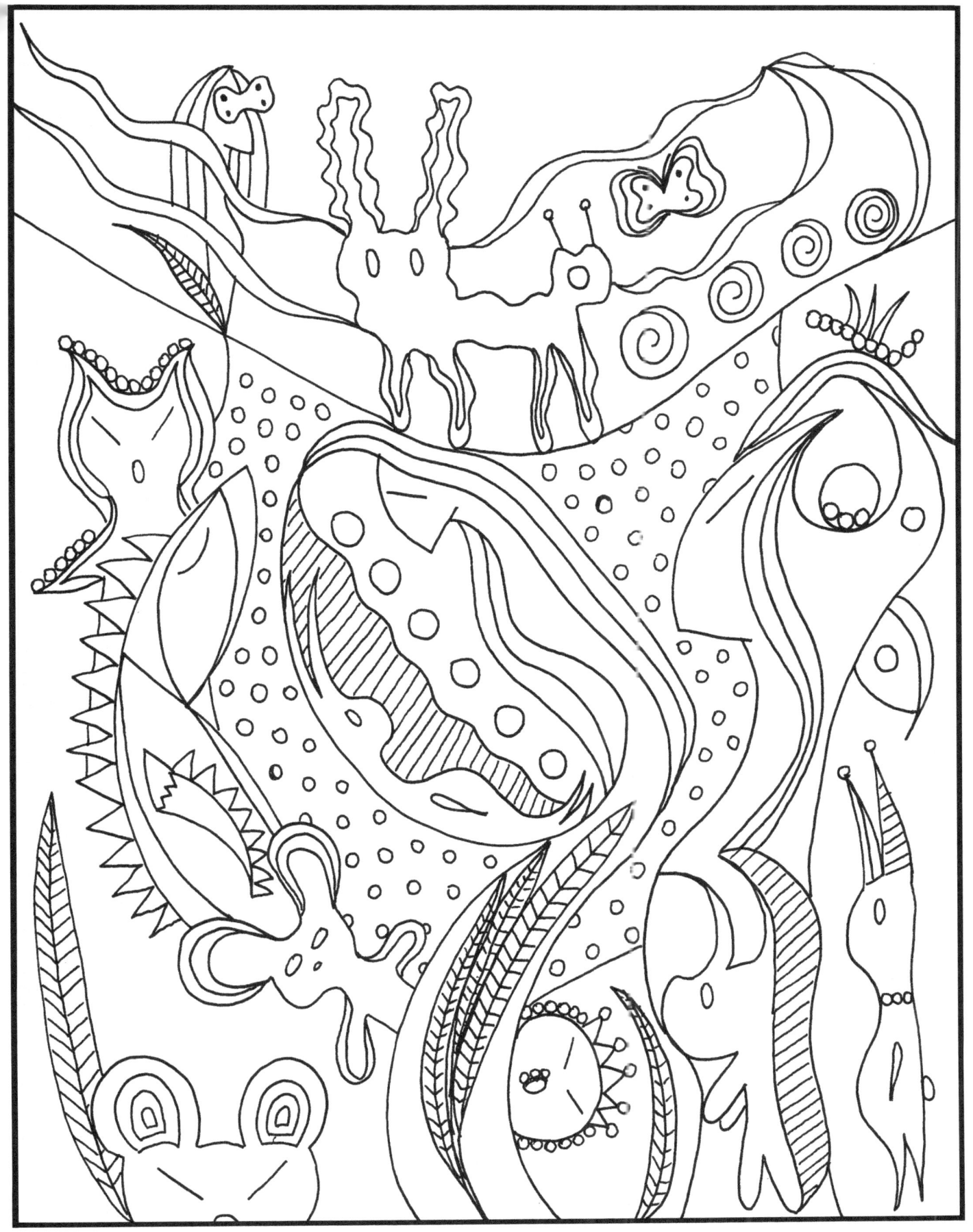

Create Your Own Secret Worlds Title
Plate Number: 07

Submit your colorful creation
to be displayed online at
www.HunterCole.org/color

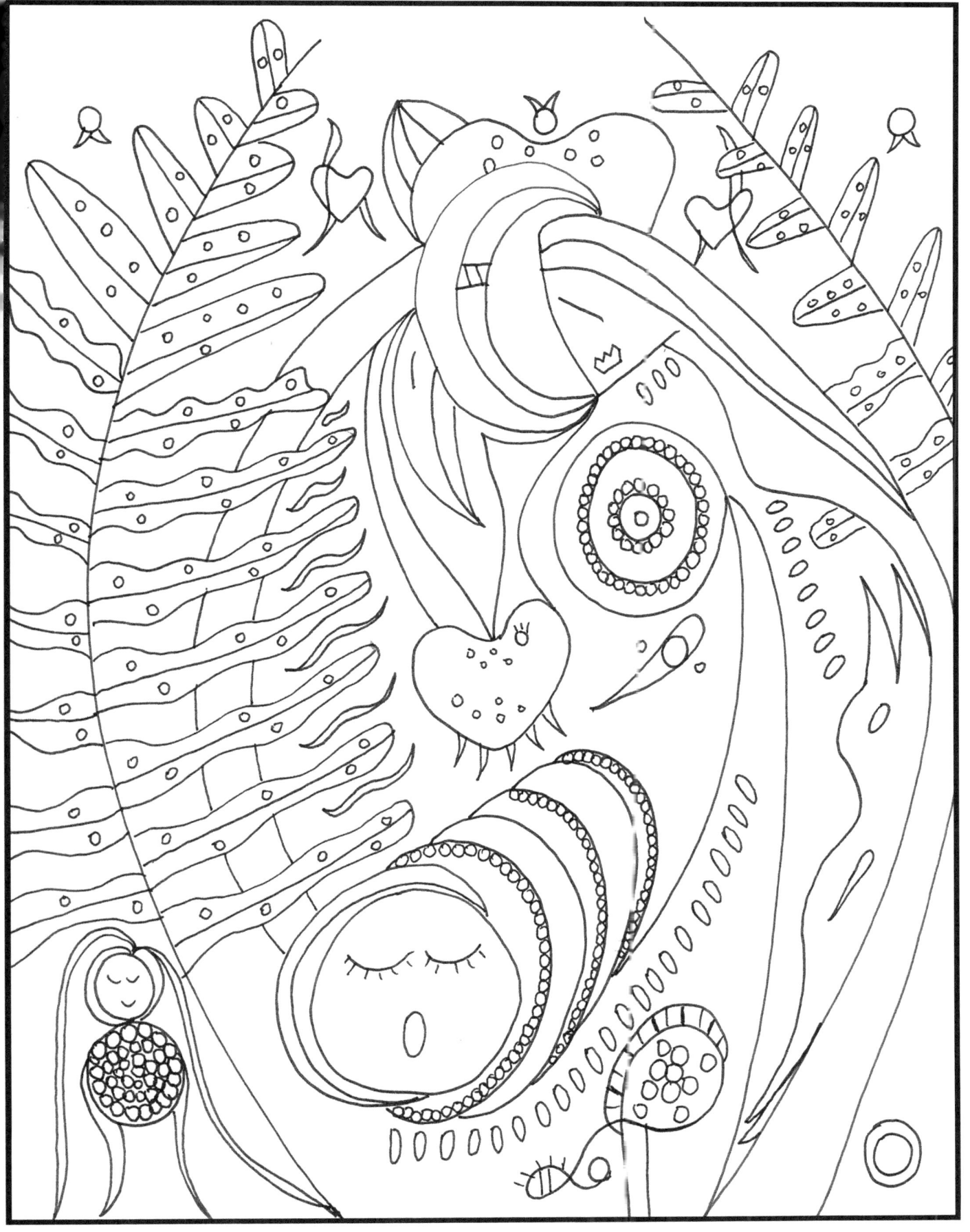

Create Your Own Secret Worlds Title
Plate Number: 08

Submit your colorful creation
to be displayed online at
www.HunterCole.org/color

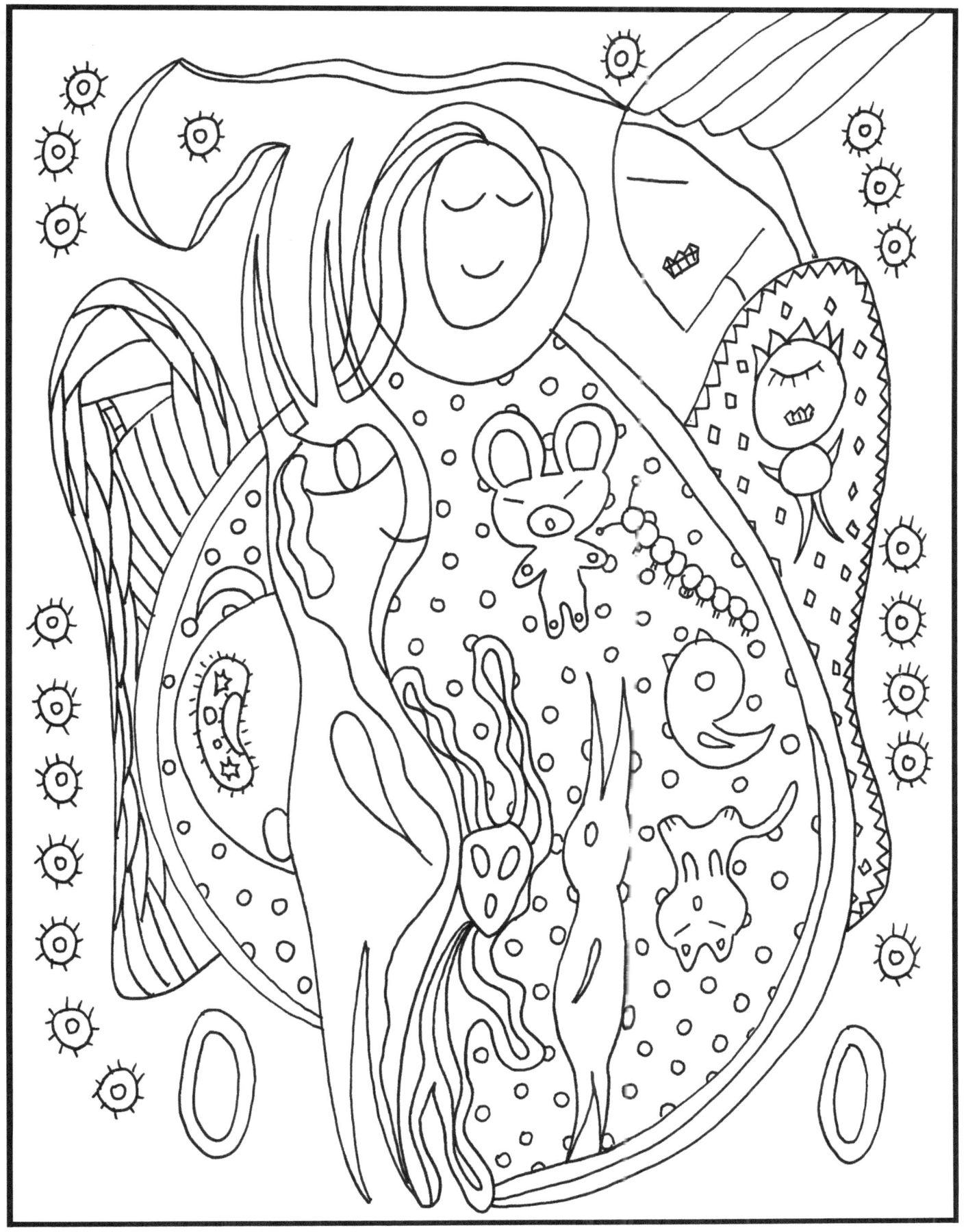

Create Your Own Secret Worlds Title
Plate Number: 09

Submit your colorful creation
to be displayed online at
www.HunterCole.org/color

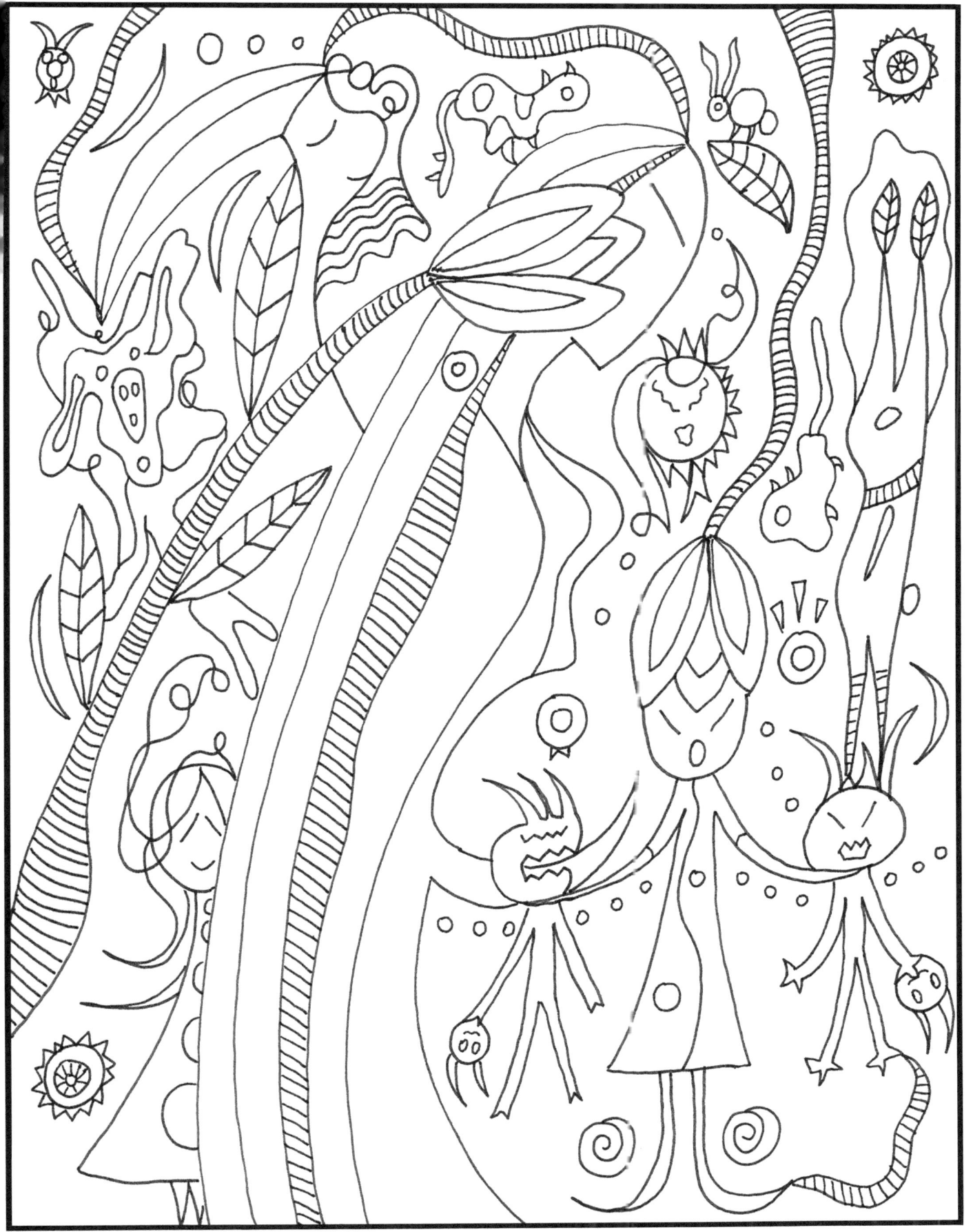

Create Your Own Secret Worlds Title
Plate Number: 10

Submit your colorful creation
to be displayed online at
www.HunterCole.org/color

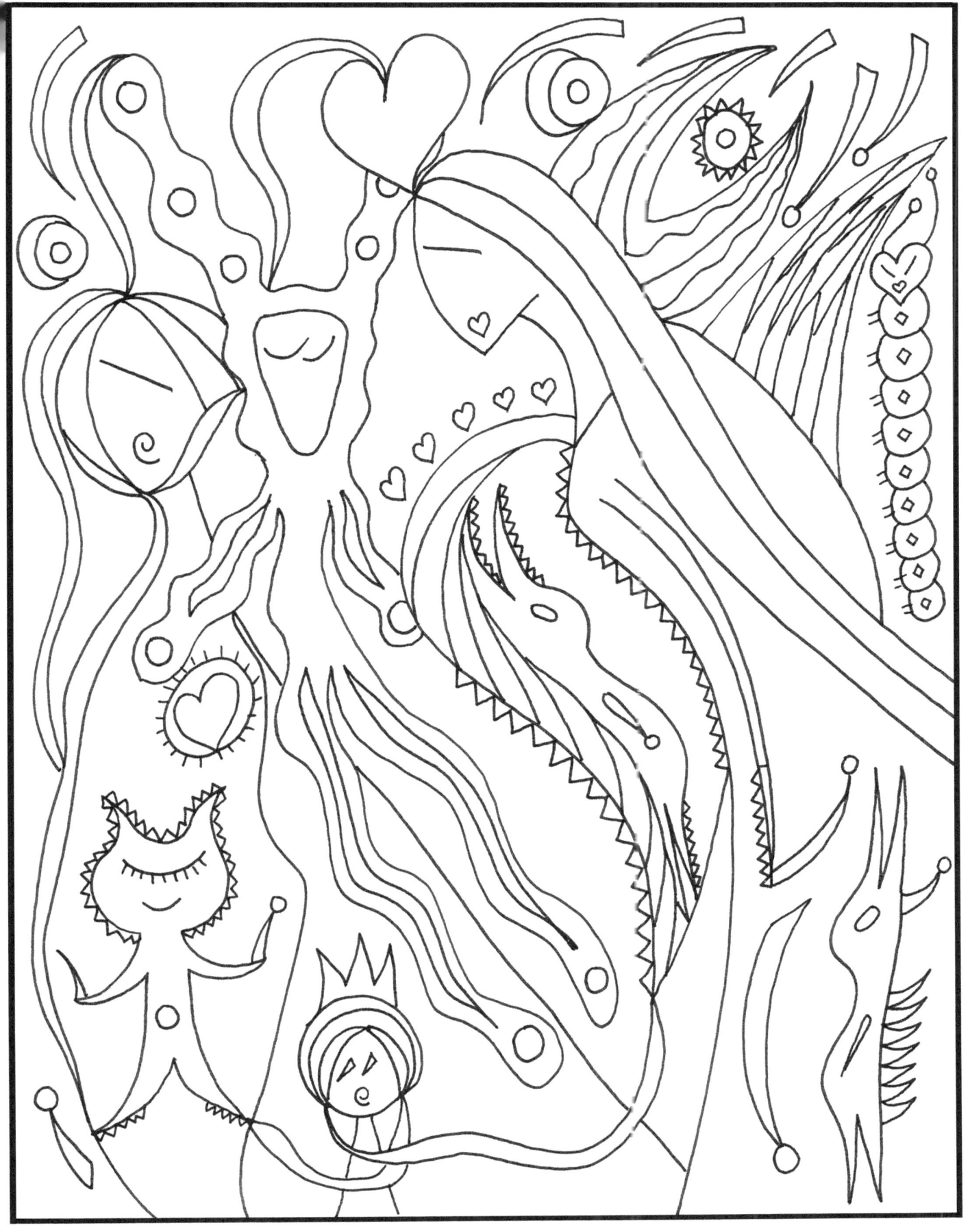

Create Your Own Secret Worlds Title
Plate Number: 11

Submit your colorful creation
to be displayed online at
www.HunterCole.org/color

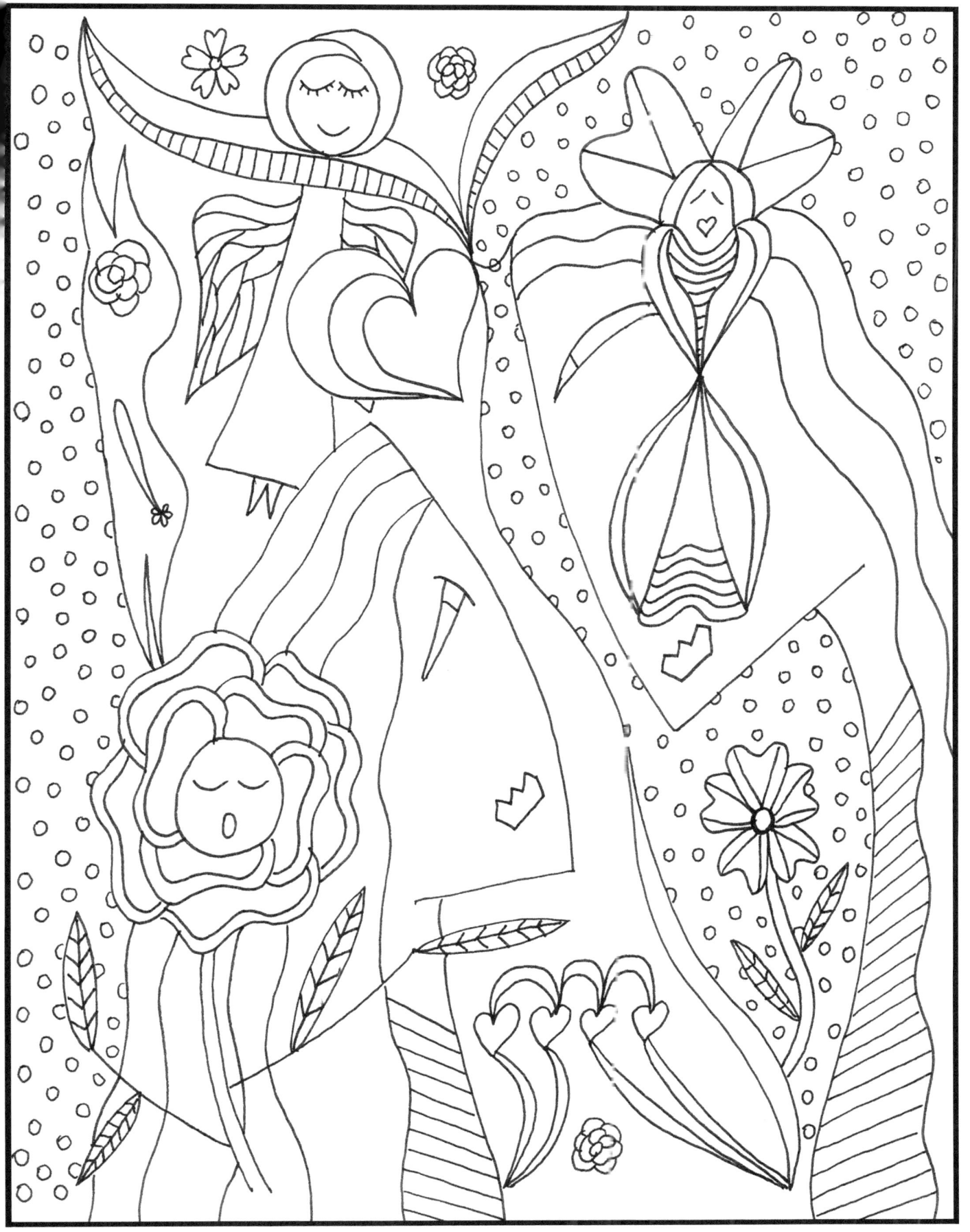

Create Your Own Secret Worlds Title
Plate Number: 12

Submit your colorful creation
to be displayed online at
www.HunterCole.org/color

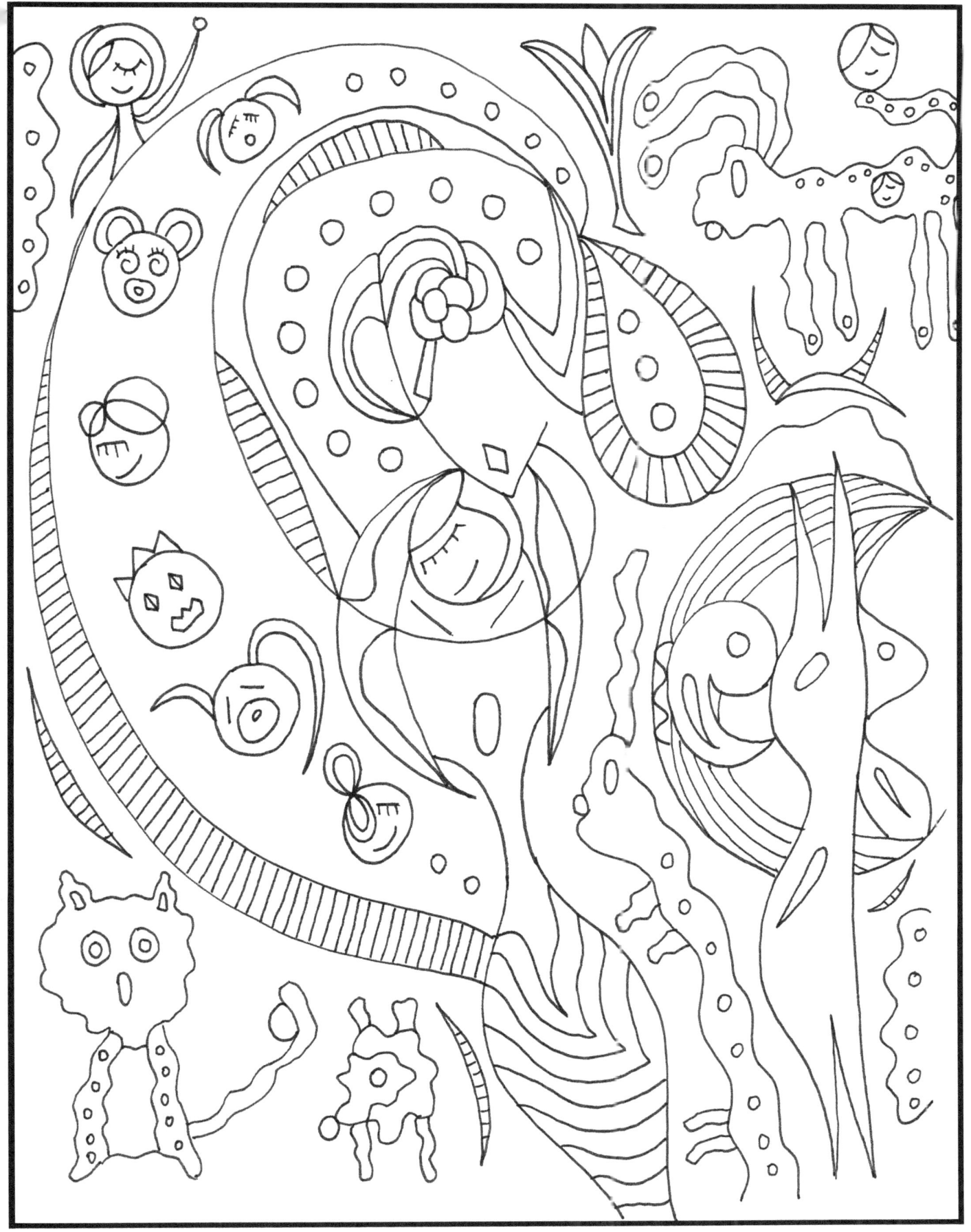

Create Your Own Secret Worlds Title

Plate Number: 13
Submit your colorful creation
to be displayed online at
www.HunterCole.org/color

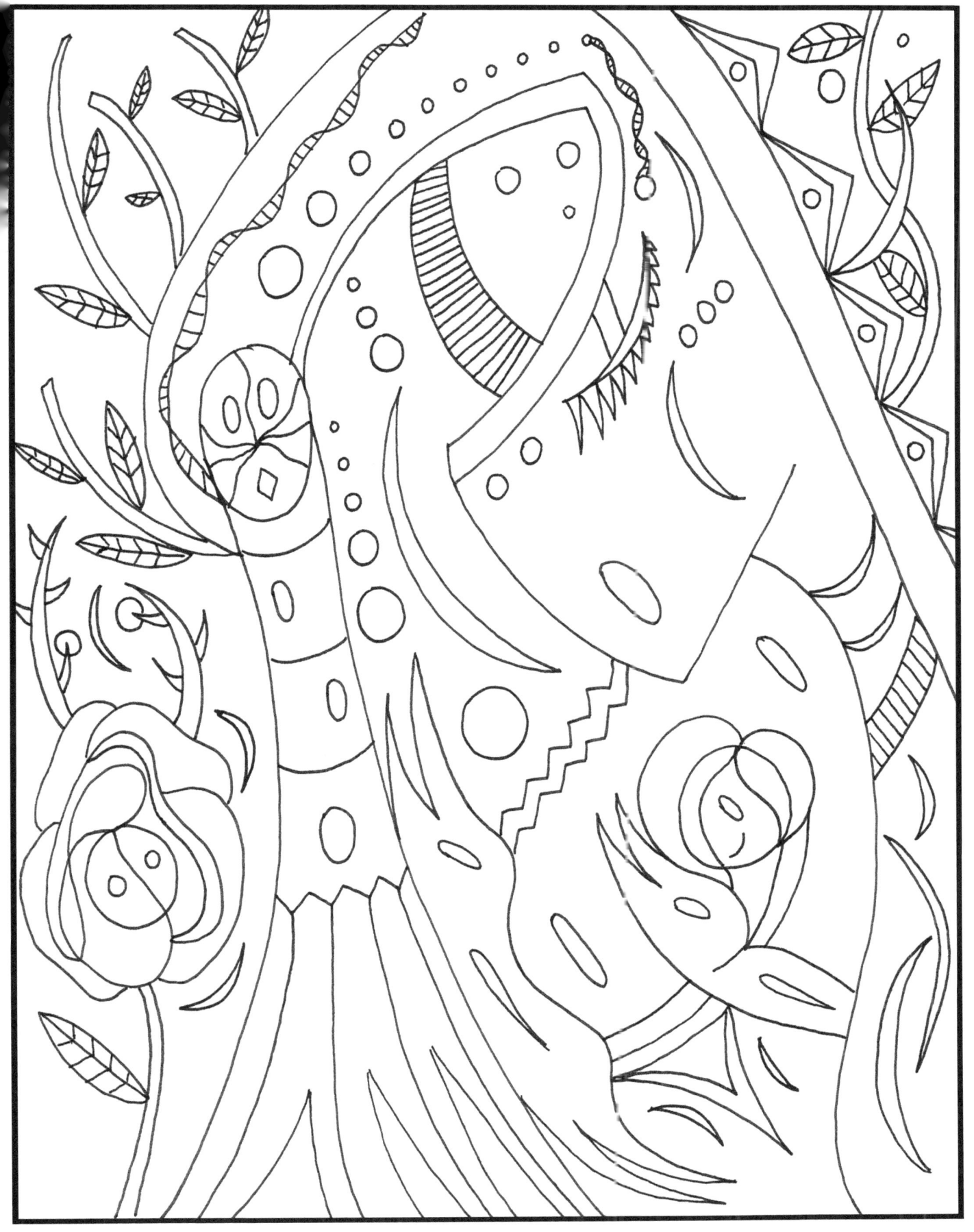

Create Your Own Secret Worlds Title
Plate Number: 14

Submit your colorful creation
to be displayed online at
www.HunterCole.org/color

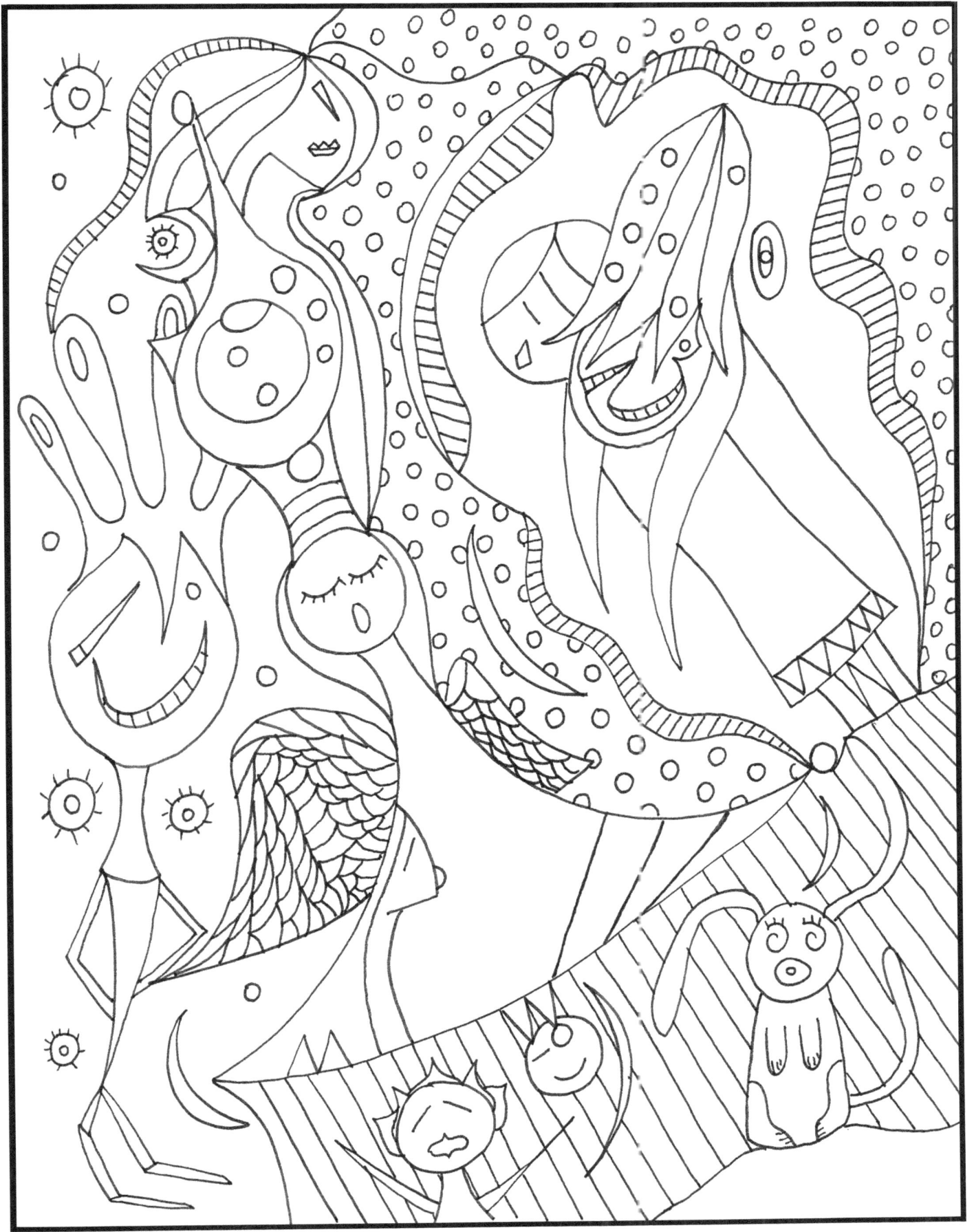

Create Your Own Secret Worlds Title
Plate Number: 15

Submit your colorful creation
to be displayed online at
www.HunterCole.org/color

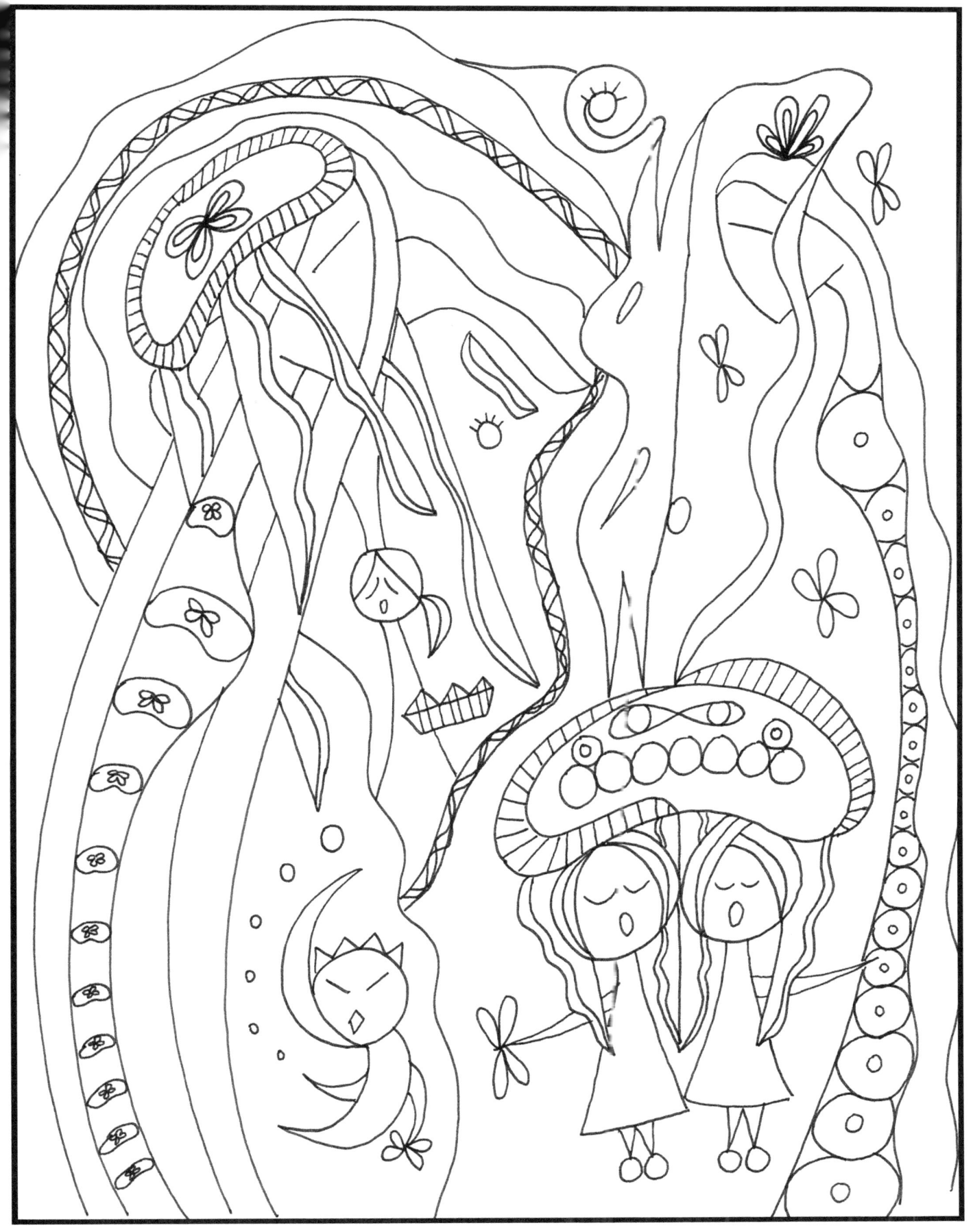

Create Your Own Secret Worlds Title
Plate Number: 16

Submit your colorful creation
to be displayed online at
www.HunterCole.org/color

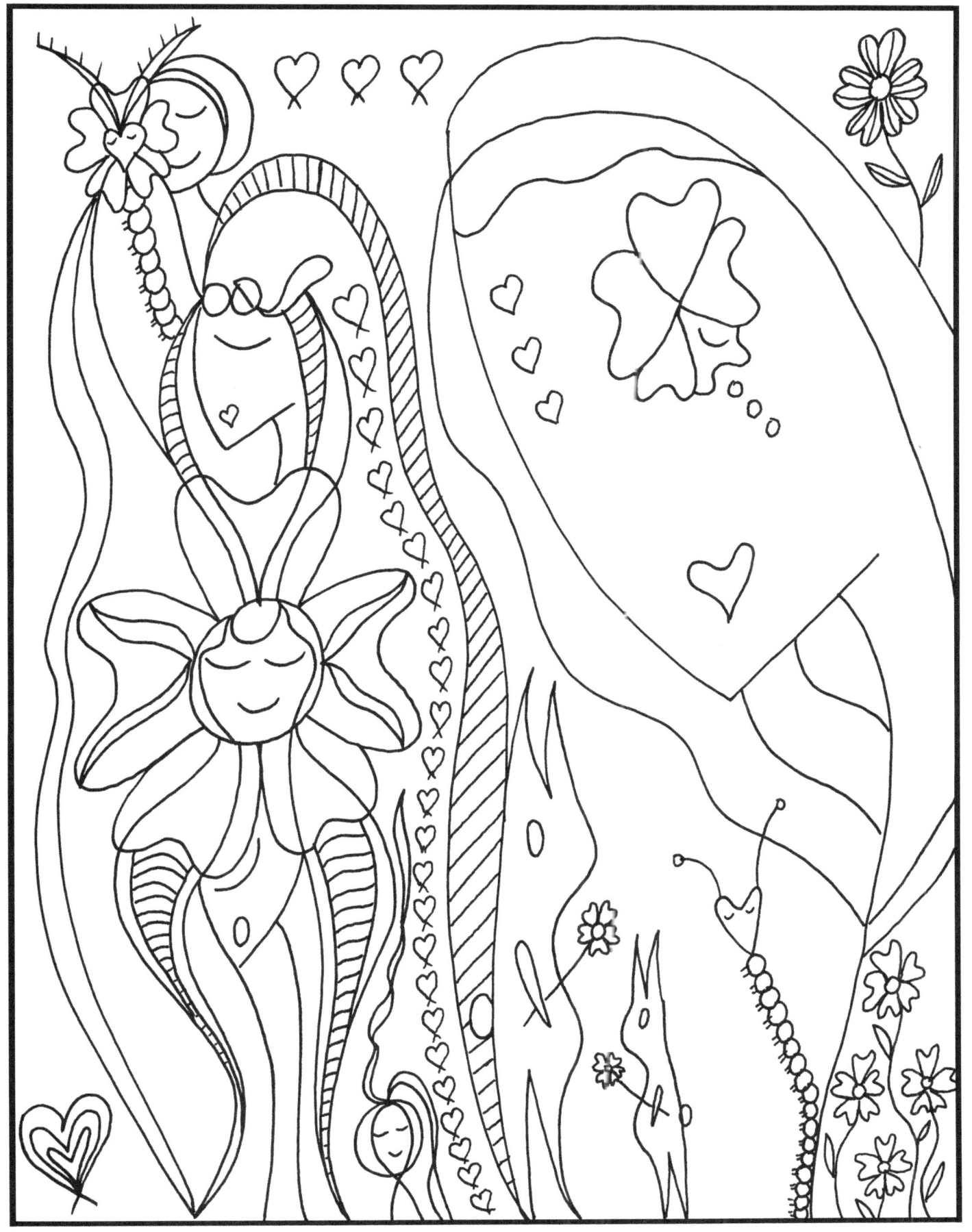

Create Your Own Secret Worlds Title
Plate Number: 17

Submit your colorful creation
to be displayed online at
www.HunterCole.org/color

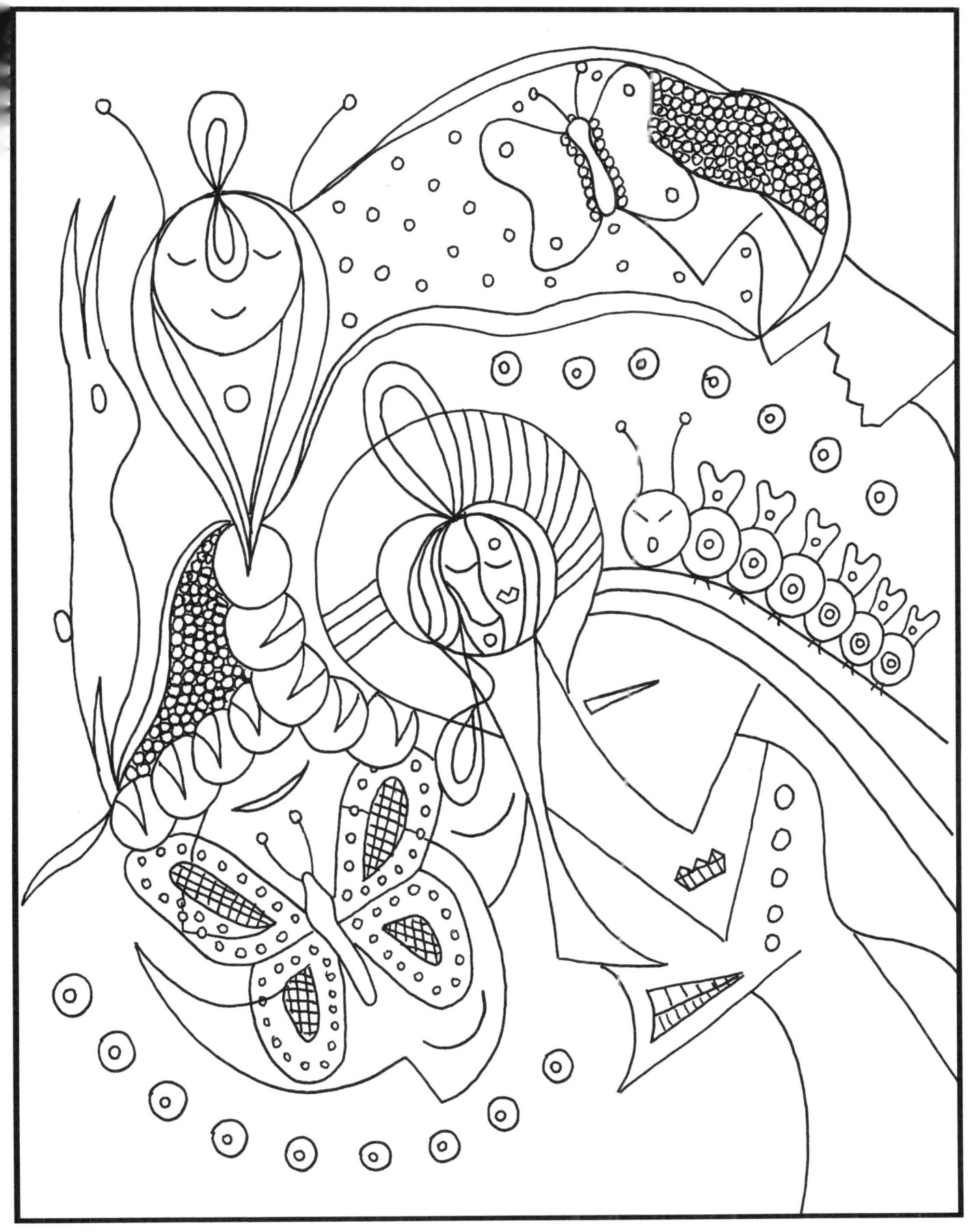

Create Your Own Secret Worlds Title
Plate Number: 18

Submit your colorful creation
to be displayed online at
www.HunterCole.org/color

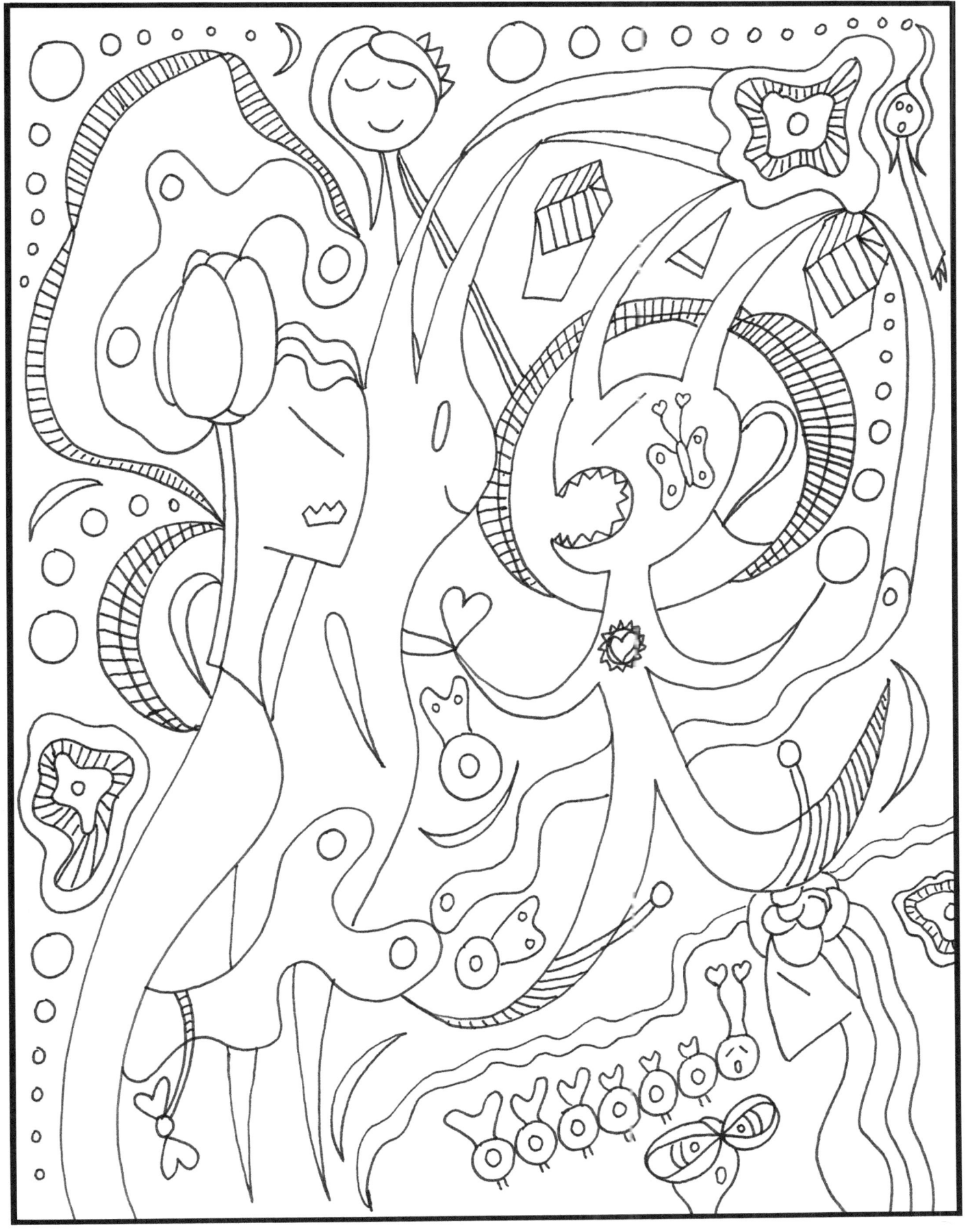

Create Your Own Secret Worlds Title
Plate Number: 19

Submit your colorful creation
to be displayed online at
www.HunterCole.org/color

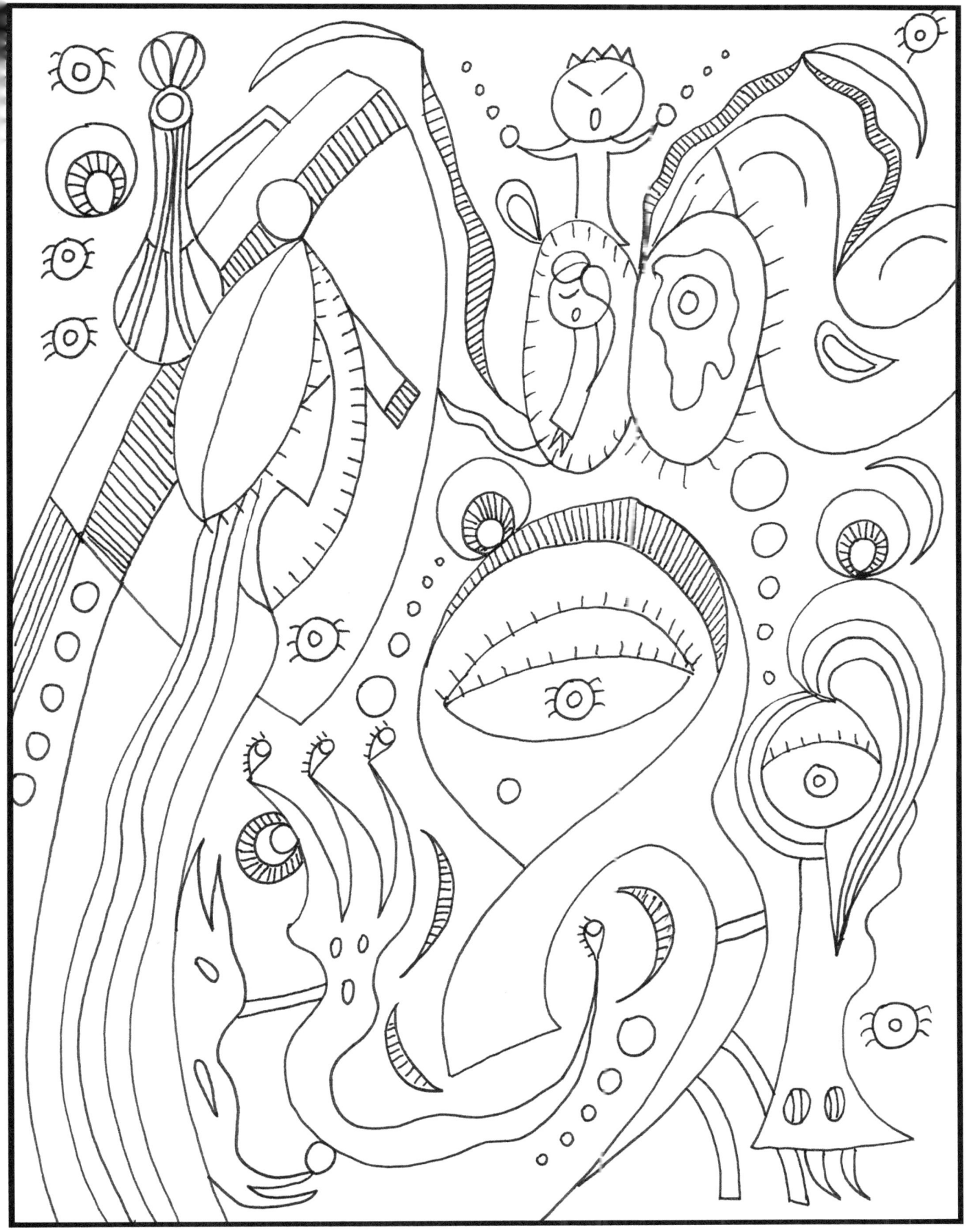

Create Your Own Secret Worlds Title
Plate Number: 20

Submit your colorful creation
to be displayed online at
www.HunterCole.org/color

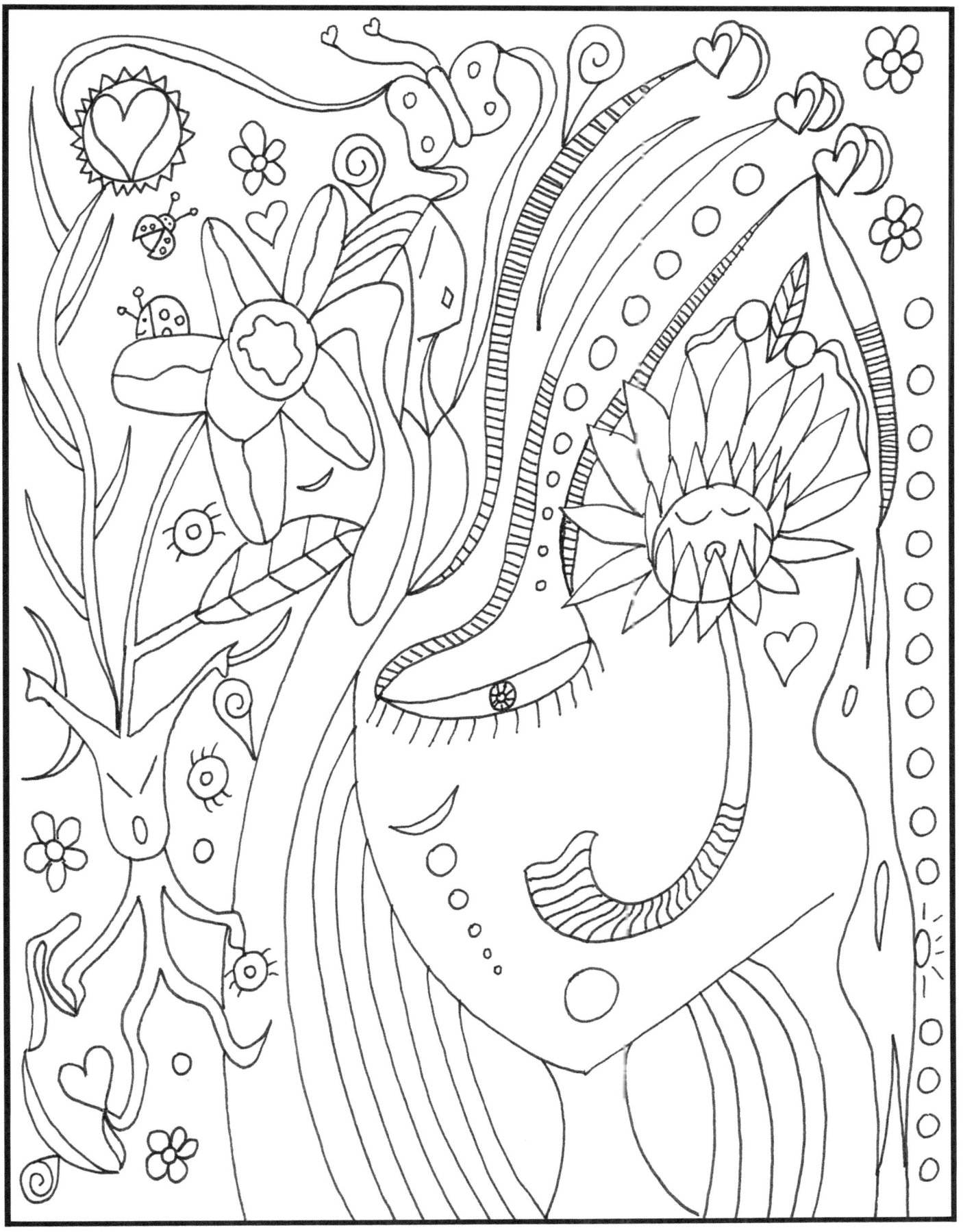

Create Your Own Secret Worlds Title
Plate Number: 21

Submit your colorful creation
to be displayed online at
www.HunterCole.org/color

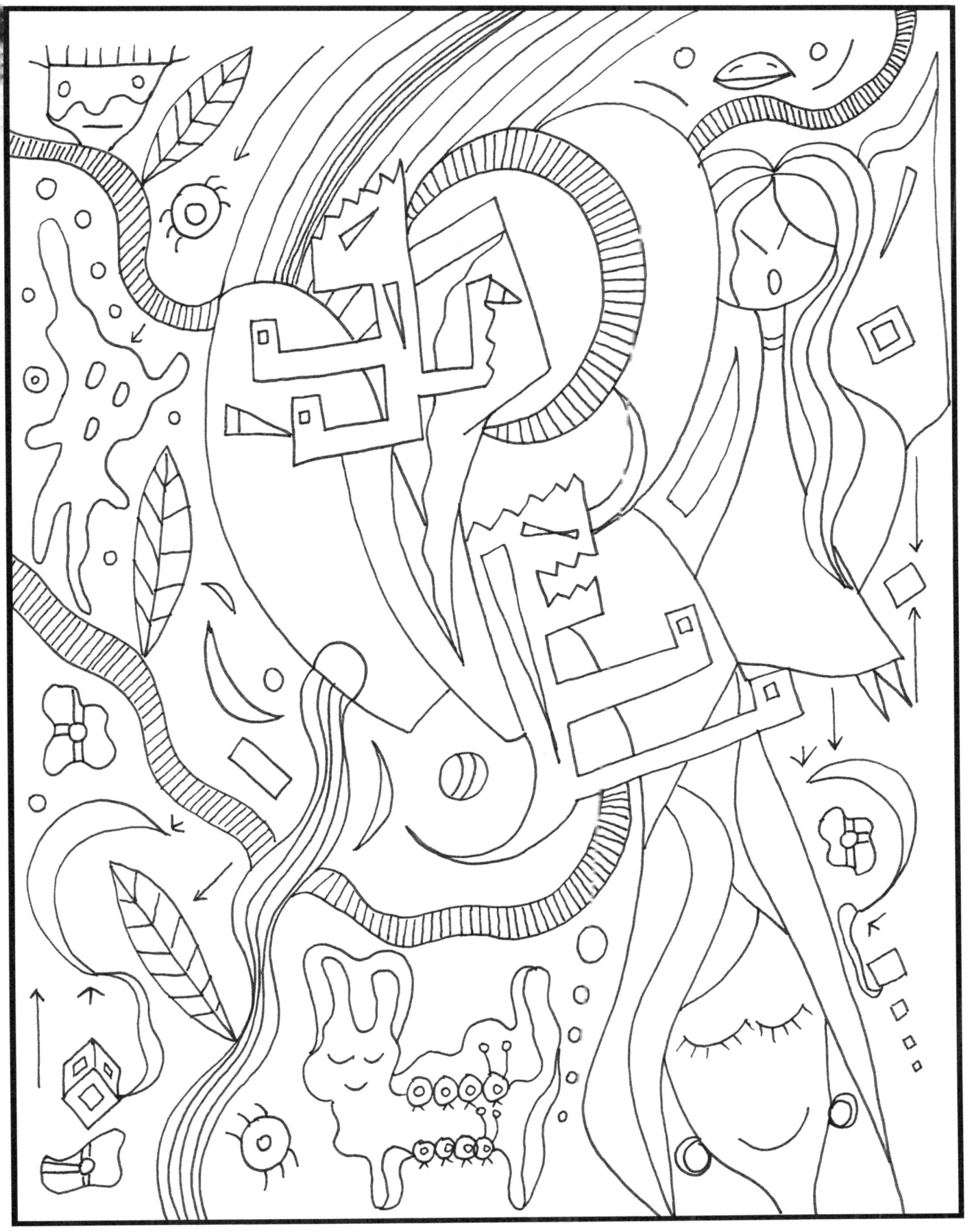

Create Your Own Secret Worlds Title
Plate Number: 22

Submit your colorful creation
to be displayed online at
www.HunterCole.org/color

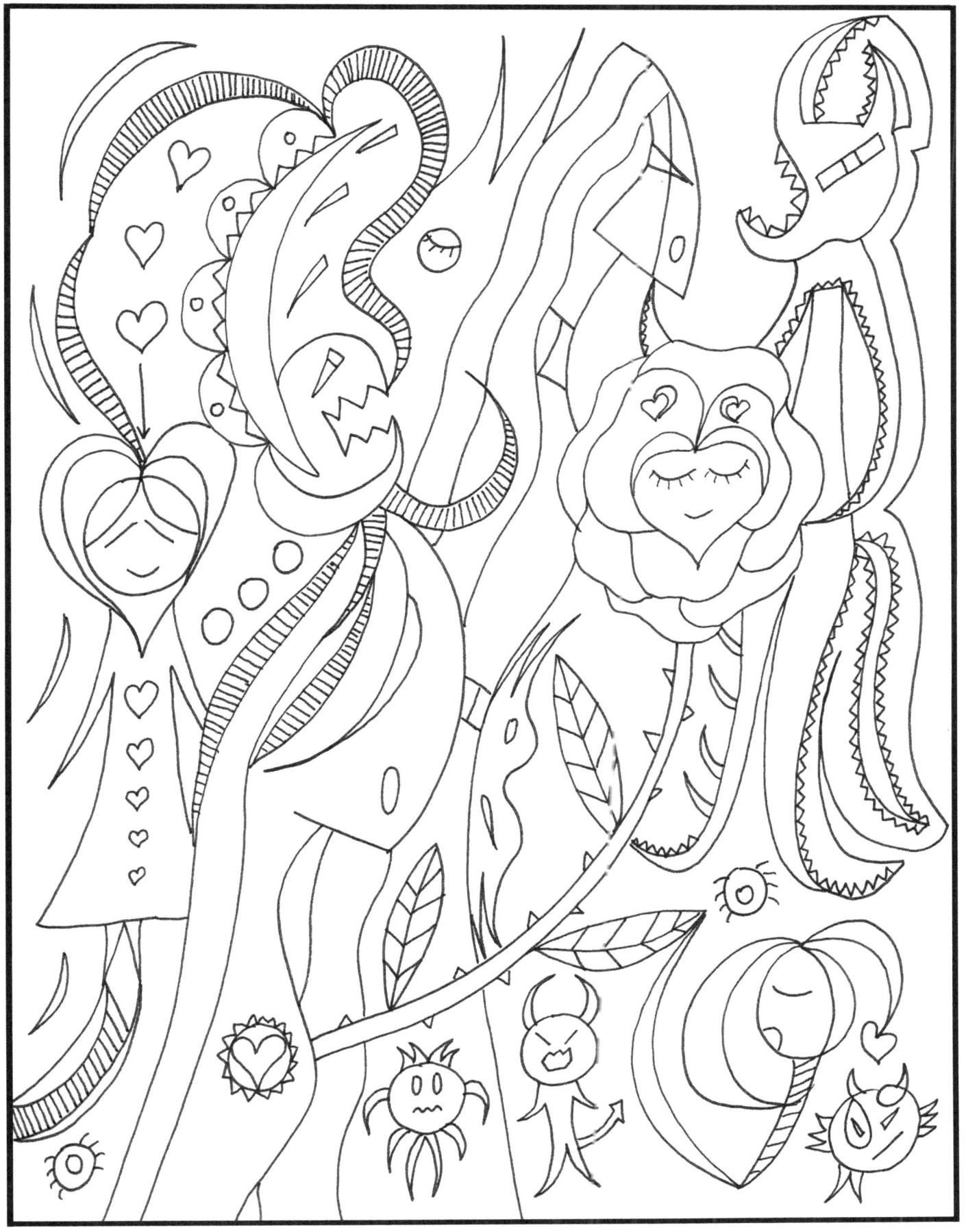

Create Your Own Secret Worlds Title
Plate Number: 23

Submit your colorful creation
to be displayed online at
www.HunterCole.org/color

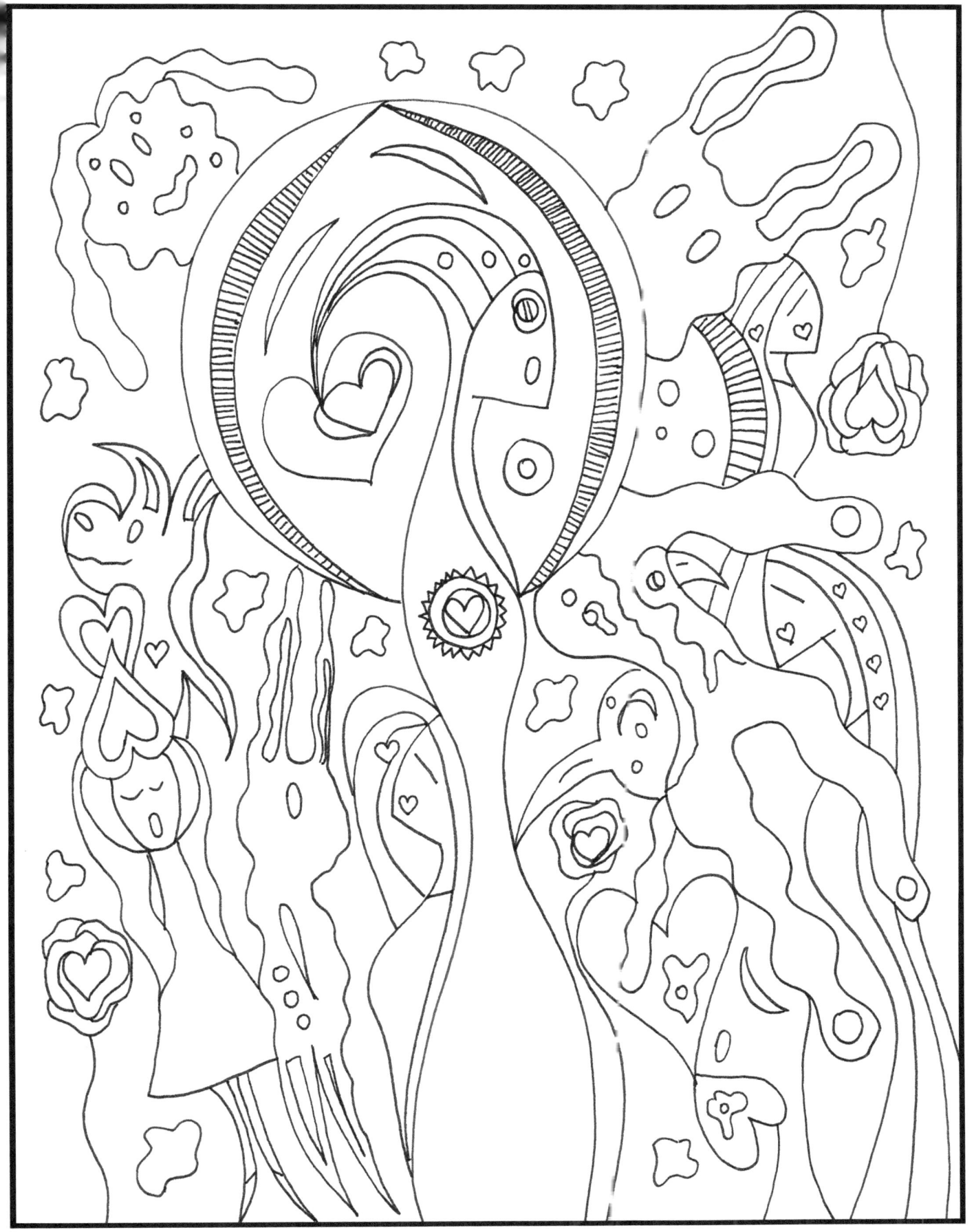

Create Your Own Secret Worlds Title
Plate Number: 24

Submit your colorful creation
to be displayed online at
www.HunterCole.org/color

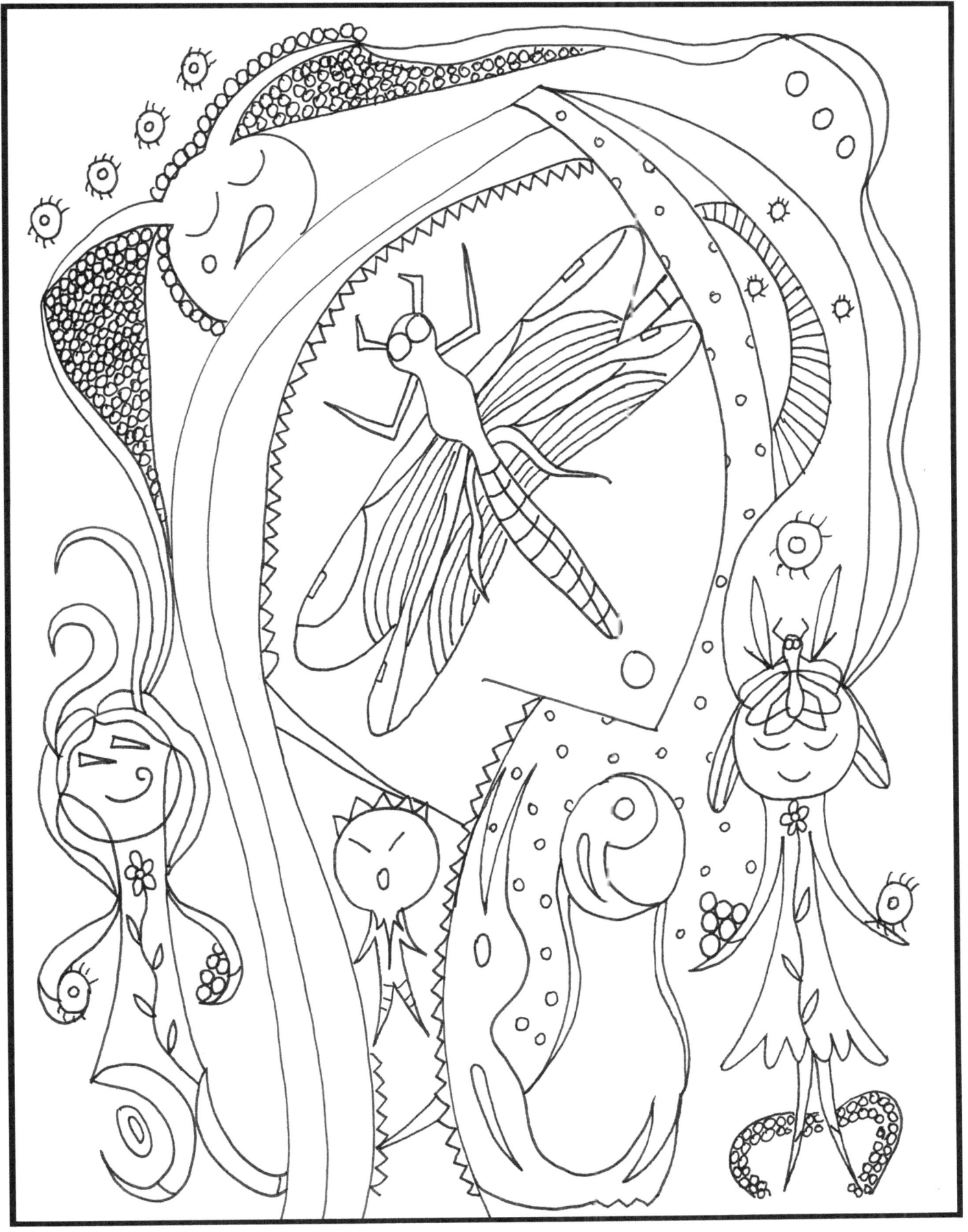

Create Your Own Secret Worlds Title
Plate Number: 25

Submit your colorful creation
to be displayed online at
www.HunterCole.org/color

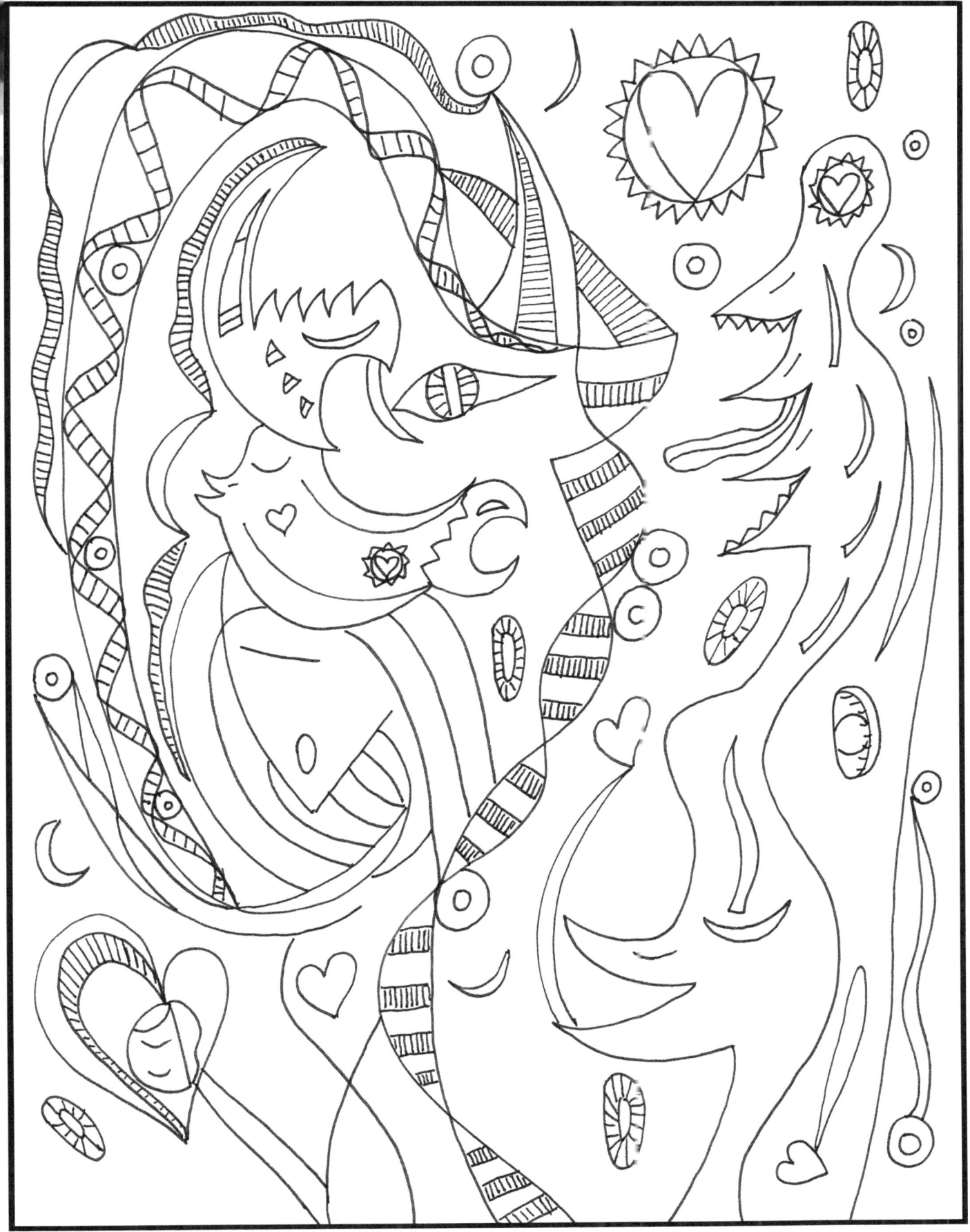

Create Your Own Secret Worlds Title
Plate Number: 26

Submit your colorful creation
to be displayed online at
www.HunterCole.org/color

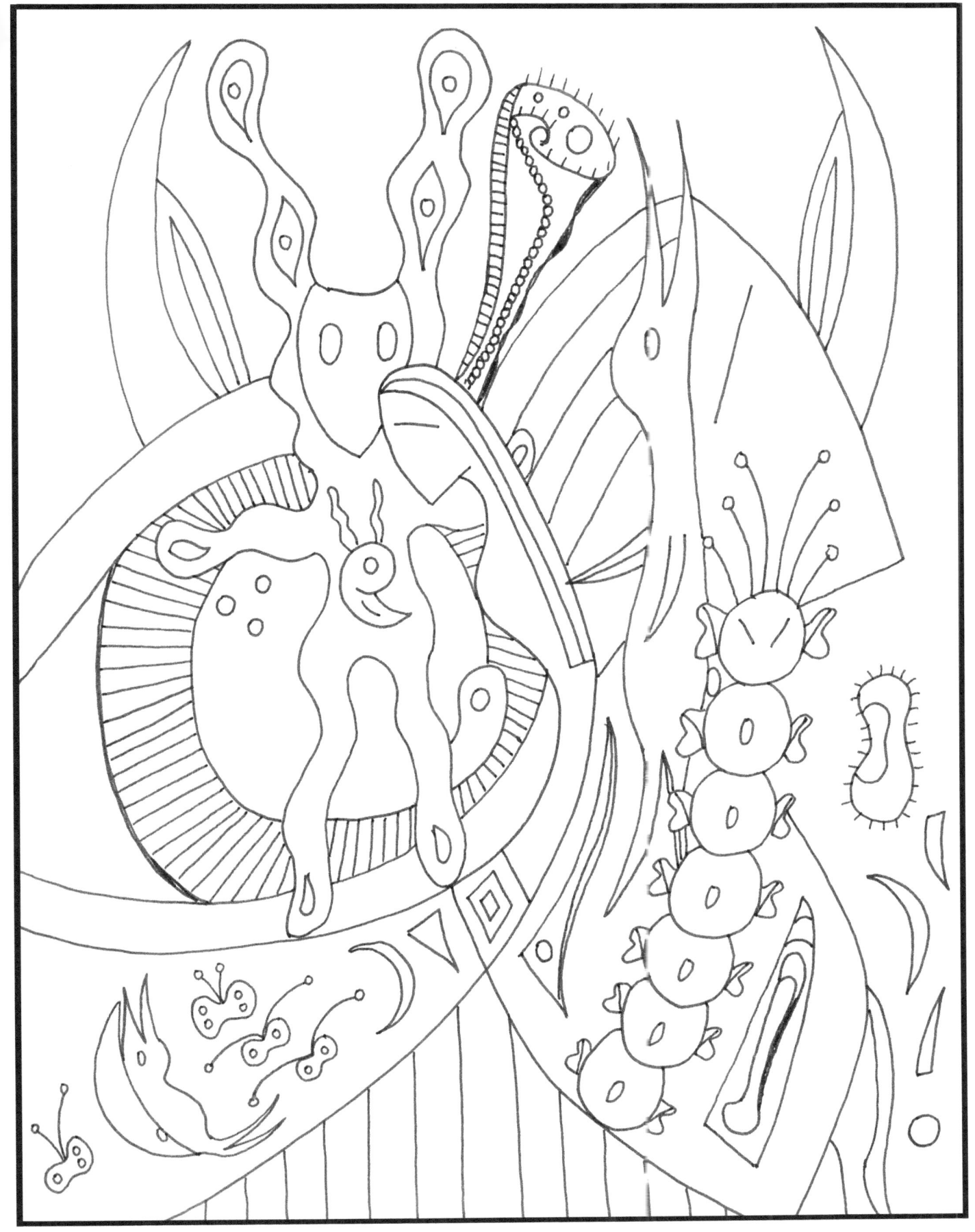

Create Your Own Secret Worlds Title
Plate Number: 27

Submit your colorful creation
to be displayed online at
www.HunterCole.org/color

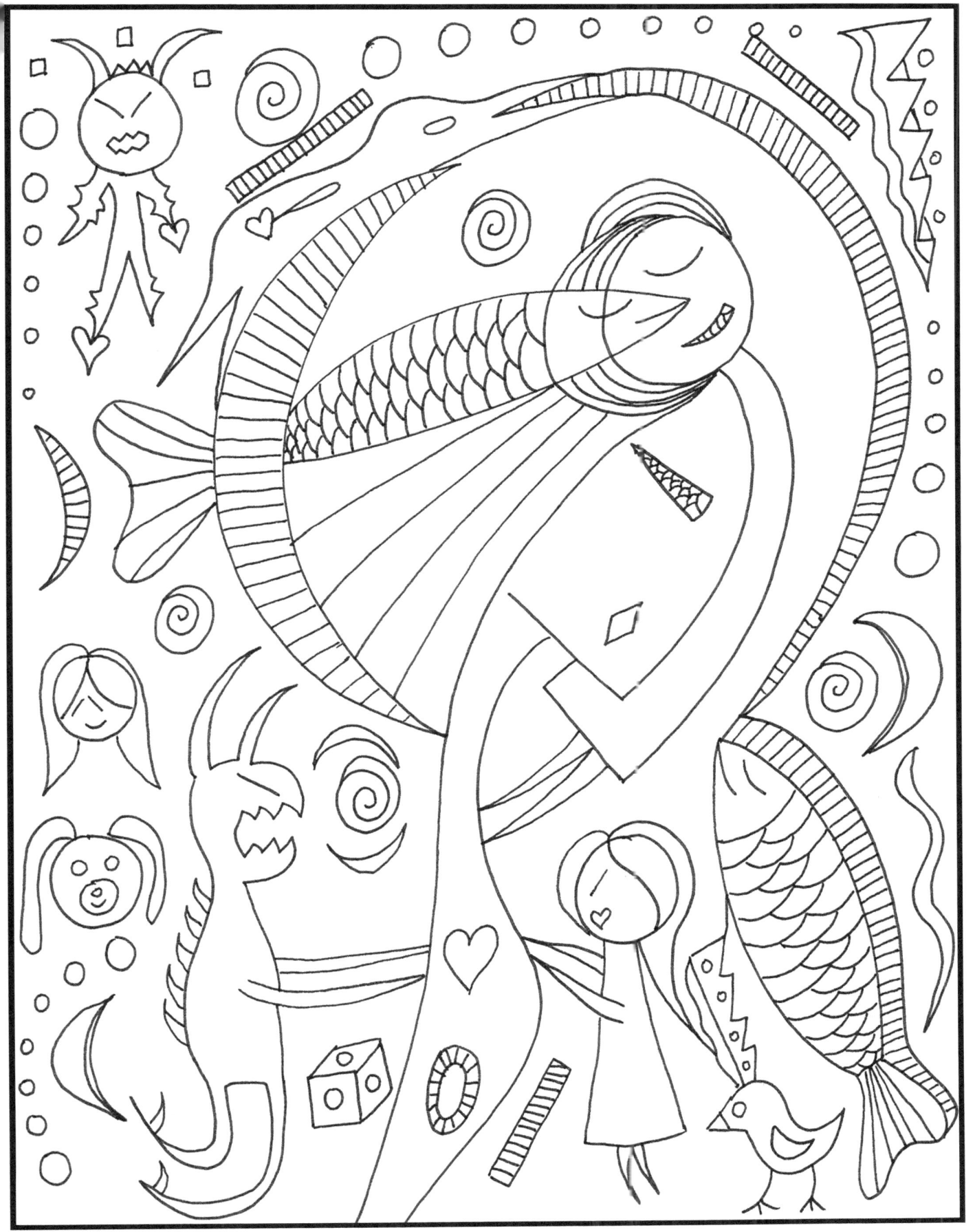

Create Your Own Secret Worlds Title
Plate Number: 28

Submit your colorful creation
to be displayed online at
www.HunterCole.org/color

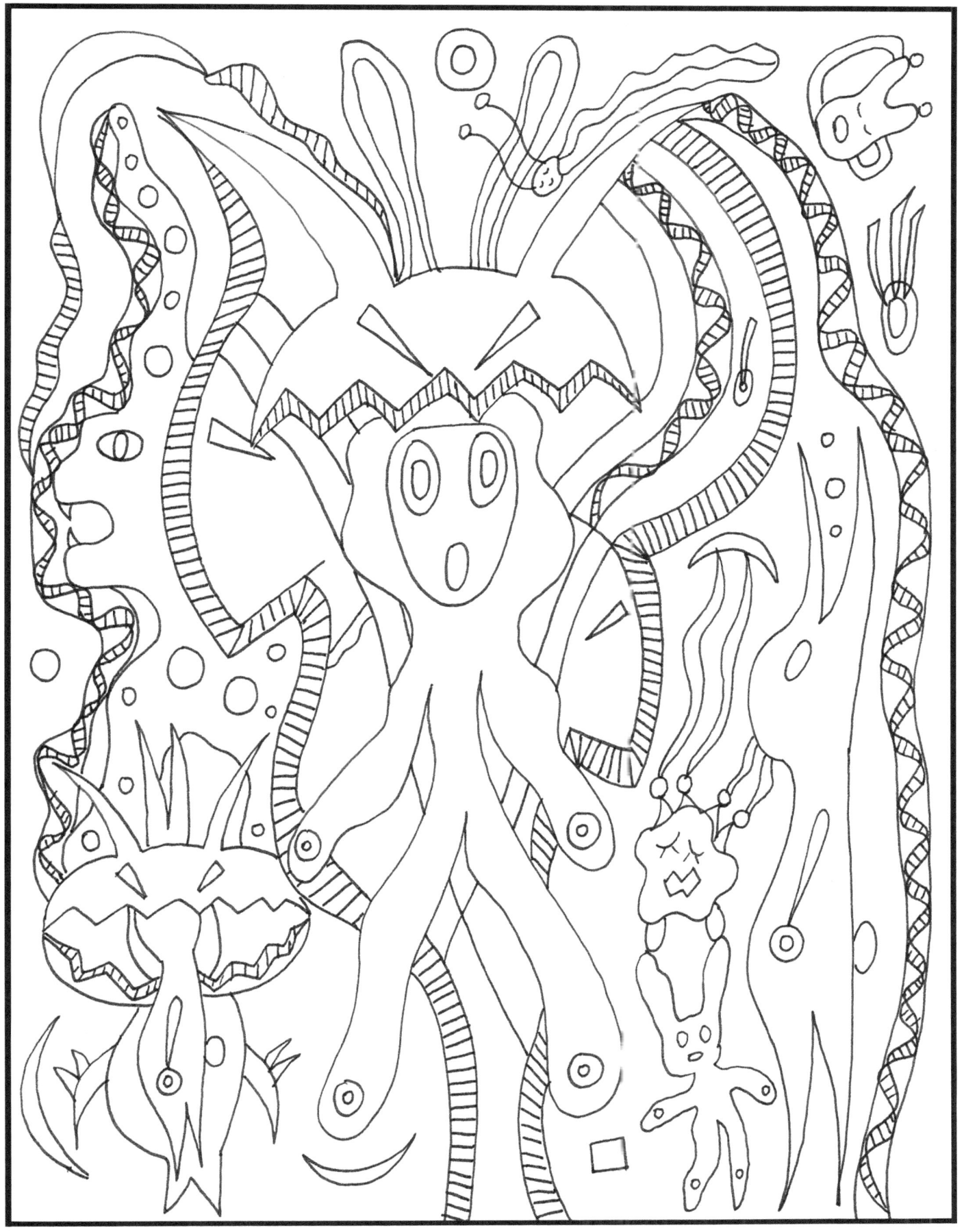

Create Your Own Secret Worlds Title
Plate Number: 29

Submit your colorful creation
to be displayed online at
www.HunterCole.org/color

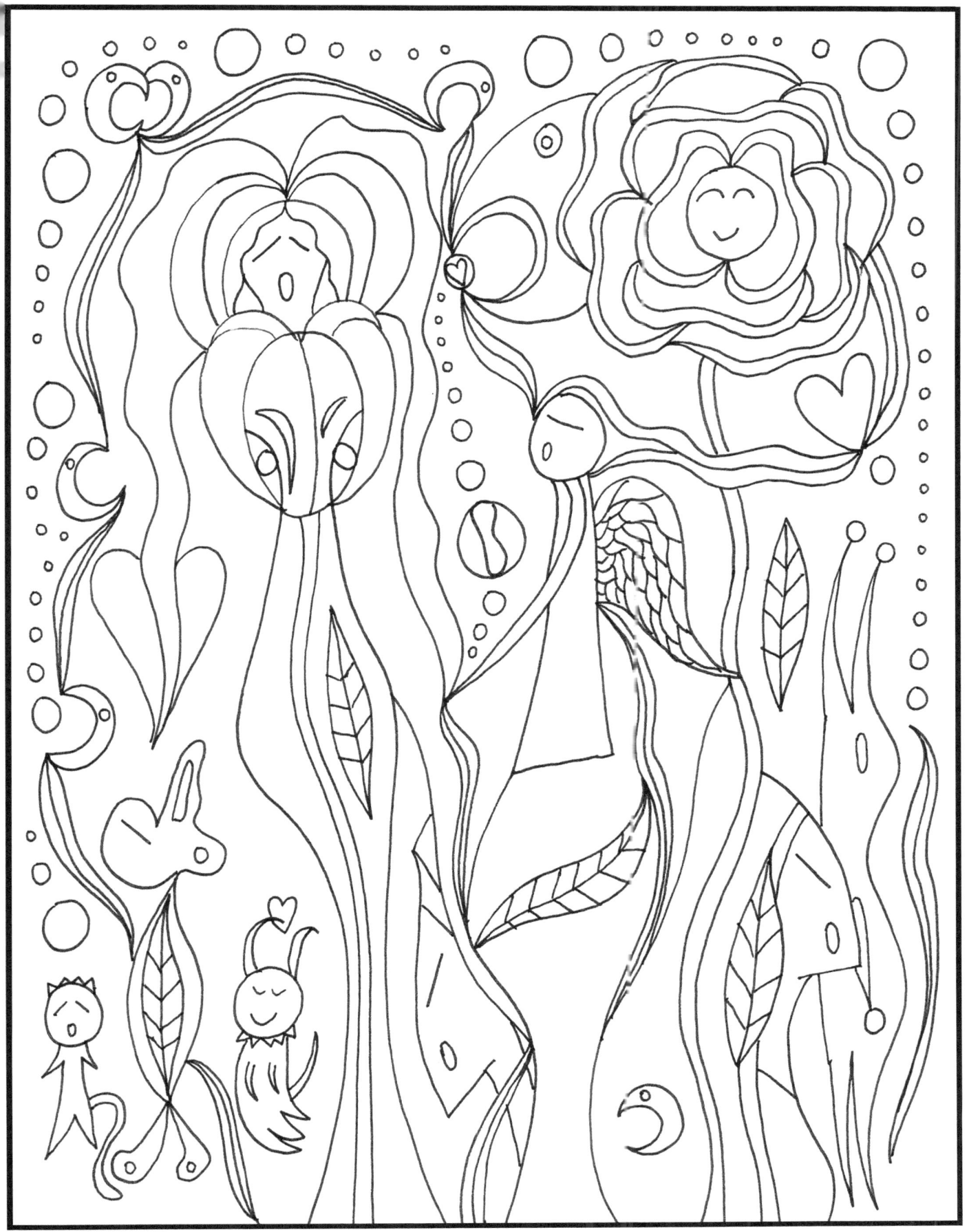

Create Your Own Secret Worlds Title
Plate Number: 30

Submit your colorful creation
to be displayed online at
www.HunterCole.org/color

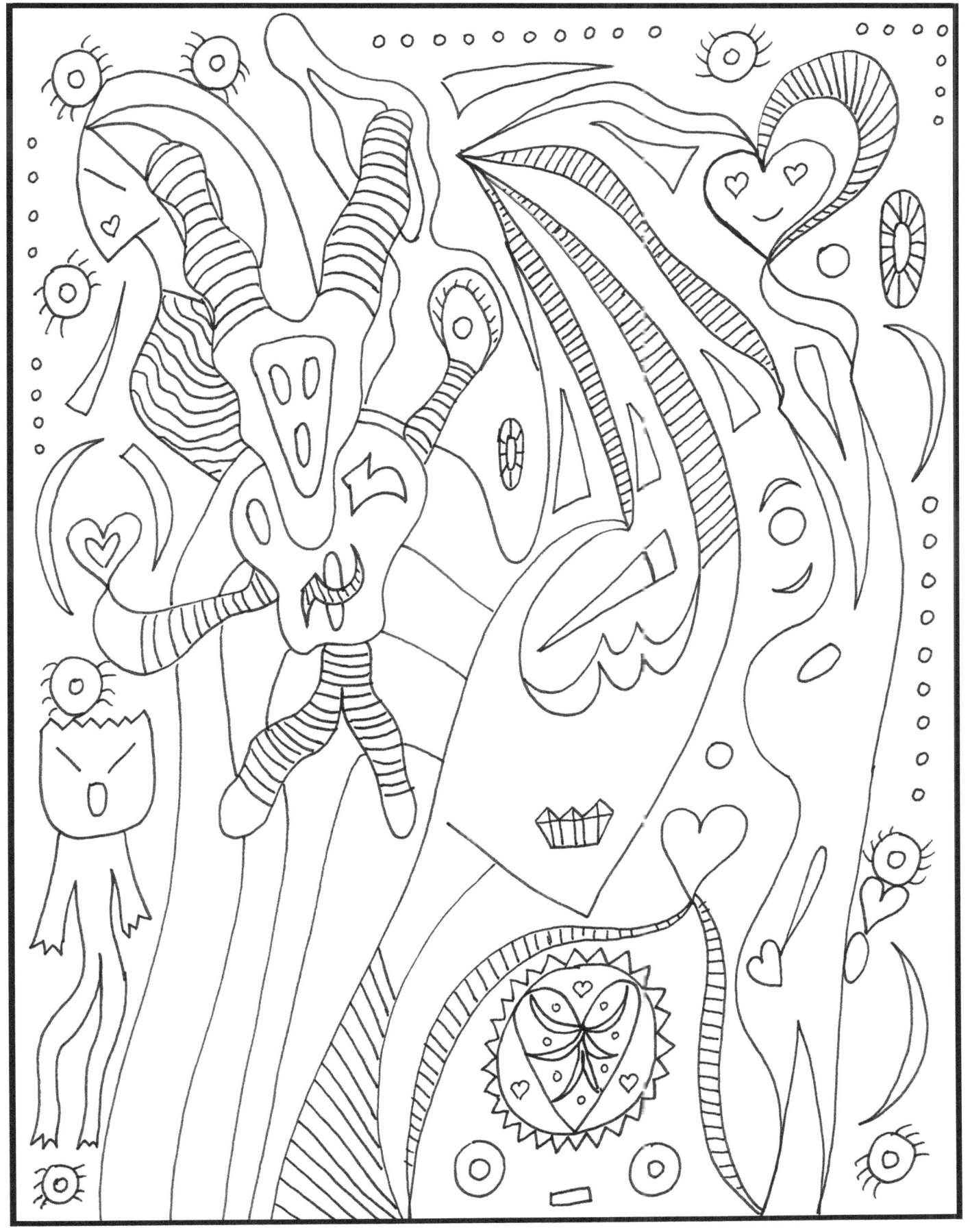

Create Your Own Secret Worlds Title
Plate Number: 31

Submit your colorful creation
to be displayed online at
www.HunterCole.org/color

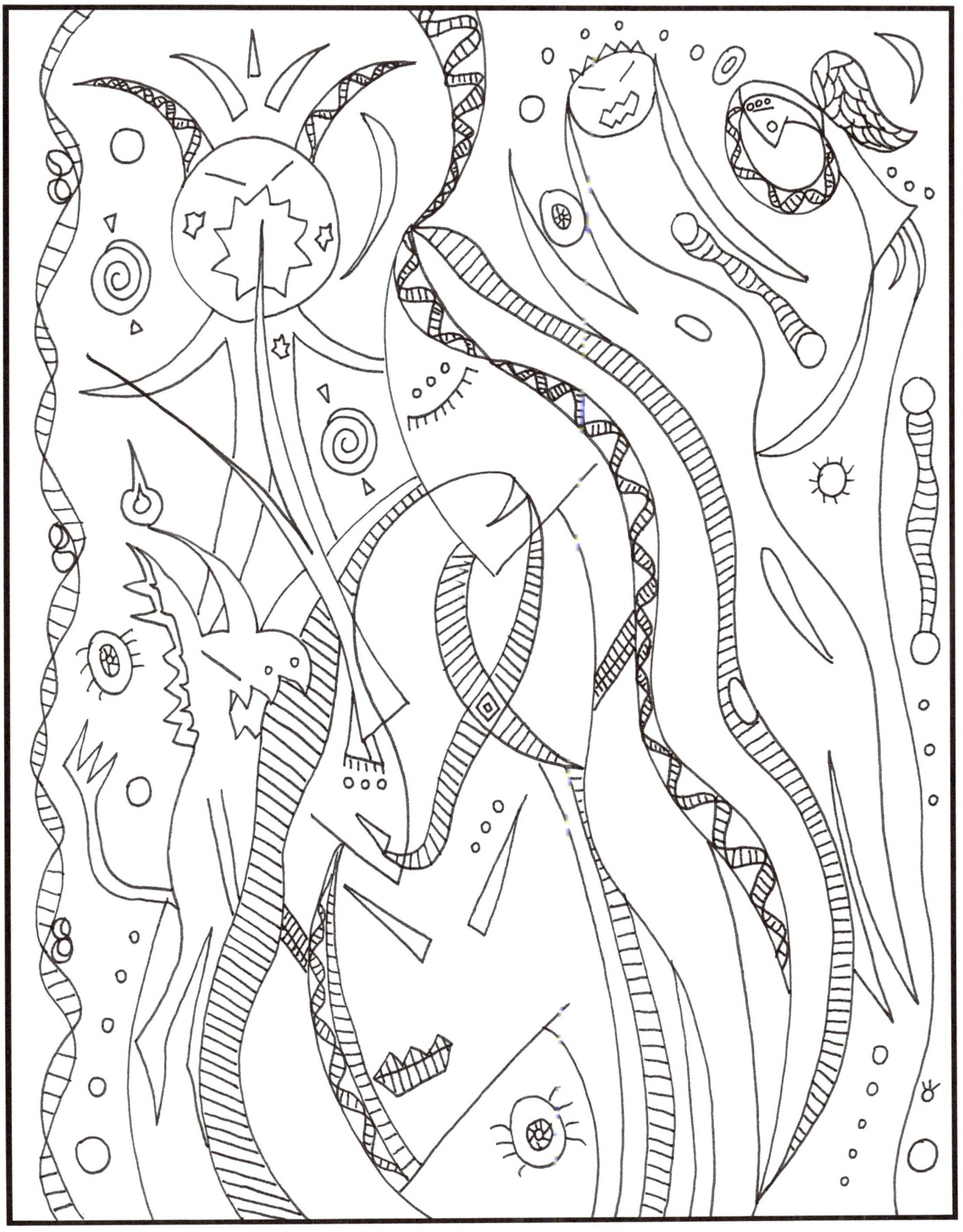

Create Your Own Secret Worlds Title
Plate Number: 32

Submit your colorful creation
to be displayed online at
www.HunterCole.org/color

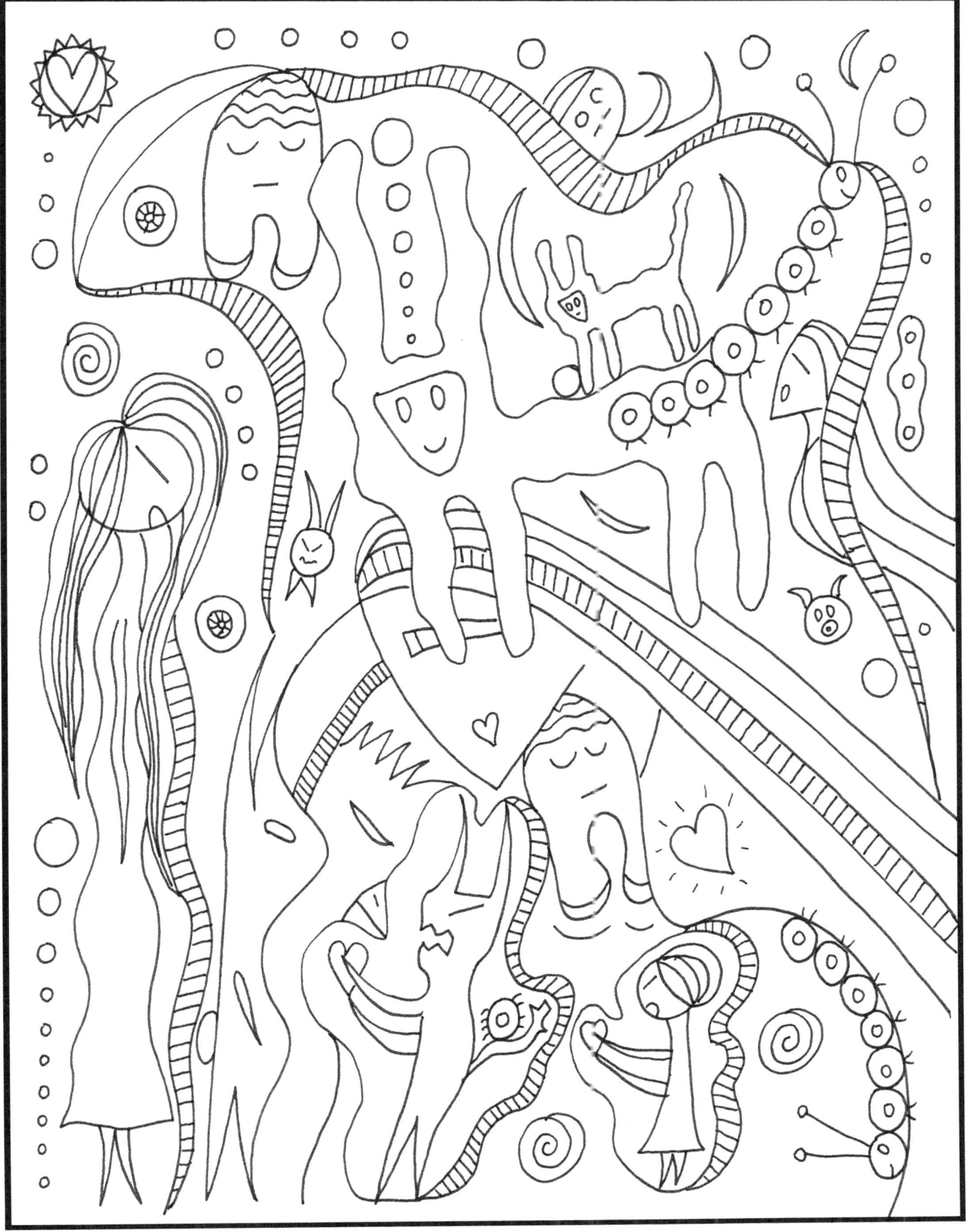

Biological Domains
installation of 14 oil paintings and LED lights
Loyola University Chicago, 2016
Hunter Cole

www.BiologicalDomains.com

Back Cover Photo Credit:
Natalie Battaglia, Loyola University Chicago

www.ingramcontent.com/pod-product-compliance
Lightning Source LLC
Chambersburg PA
CBHW080524220526
45465CB00006B/2590